# Languages of Minority

# Languages of Minority

*Orality, Translation, and Desiring English*

SOWMYA DECHAMMA CC

*Professor, Centre for Comparative Literature*
*University of Hyderabad, Hyderabad*

**OXFORD**
UNIVERSITY PRESS

# OXFORD
## UNIVERSITY PRESS

Great Clarendon Street, Oxford, OX2 6DP,
United Kingdom

Oxford University Press is a department of the University of Oxford.
It furthers the University's objective of excellence in research, scholarship,
and education by publishing worldwide. Oxford is a registered trade mark of
Oxford University Press in the UK and in certain other countries

Published in the United States of America by Oxford University Press
198 Madison Avenue, New York, NY 10016, United States of America

British Library Cataloguing in Publication Data

Data available

Library of Congress Control Number: 2024943935

ISBN 978-0-19-890845-6

DOI: 10.1093/oso/9780198908456.001.0001

Printed and bound in India by
Replika Press Pvt. Ltd.

# Preface and Acknowledgements

I have been working on this book forever. So much so that I now feel I have said and written nothing. To write a book that largely critiques the power of writing while simultaneously acknowledging its inevitable presence—in fact to recognize the enabling presence of writing today for many communities, seems contradictory, at least superficially. This adds to the contradictions that the presence of English amongst us has given rise to. It is to these contradictions and many others that surround languages and surround our lives that this book hopes to make some contribution.

At first, the book might look too scattered. Like the contradictions, there is some clarity in this scattering and I hope it opens up as the reader continues to read. This book was initially conceptualized to address only concerns around the Kodava language, a language I have inhabited throughout my life, and around English, a language that has inhabited me in more ways than Kodava. The book does retain that focus while simultaneously addressing issues that concern many languages of minority.

This work seeks to understand how the languages of minorities in India have been constructed and understood throughout colonialism and nationalist periods through to contemporary times. By using certain examples, the work also attempts to chart how concepts and practices of orality and writing, the concept of vernacular, the thought and act of translation are crucial in our understanding of languages. More importantly, the work points to different axes of power that (un)make language communities. The work also presents how the role of English is complex and perhaps the desire for English needs to be understood differently for minoritized people.

What I wish the book to do is to question prevalent notions around multilinguality, connect notions of multilinguality and that of mother tongues to the acts of power, map how orality in the Indian context needs to be understood differently in its connection to writing, vernacular, and history proper. The book argues that communities that are invested with the power of writing actively construct notions around language and these have certain implications for the languages of the minority, including the ways in which negotiations and resistances emerge.

Too many friends have contributed to this—through their work, through love, and through care. My gratitude to:

Manohar, in the hope that his wonderful work will be out soon. Manohar who said: 'mine will never be done, but you are not done?'.

Susie Tharu whose 'Do not wait for the work to be perfect' did it.

David Goldberg to whom I was trying to explain what I do and he simply put it this way 'so you work on language and politics?'.

Shafeeq, for his friendship and also for carefully reading whatever I sent him.

Asha Singh, whose one observation on my work kind of shaped this book.

Probal, for the mentor he is.

For the anonymous reviewers who were so thorough. If the book does not address the concerns they raised, it is because I could not stay with it any longer.

Sreebitha, Shan, Lenny, Barath, Vellai, Bipin, Viju, Yogitha—fellow travellers in pretty much everything.

Sathyaprakash, for our earlier work together, which I think made us believe in ourselves.

Mary, Minu, Shilpaa, Comrade, Sununda, Vishnu—for always being there, for listening/reading, for bearing with me patiently . . . not to mention the warmth of our friendship.

Ravindra and Geetika—for dreaming for me.

My undercurrent friends who sustain me in more ways than one.

My colleagues at the Centre for Comparative Literature and office staff deserve a huge thanks.

Colleagues at Queens College, City University of New York, especially Chris, Ali, and Clare for sharing their time, thoughts, and love.

United States-India Educational Foundation (USIEF) and Fulbright, which allowed me time to write much of this during the harrowing time in New York during Covid 2019.

All my MA students and PhDs—they listened to me and to my ideas in different courses I taught, in different conversations we have had. If this book is worth something, it is because of their discussions, insights, and the interest they have shown.

Diwakar, who has read every line of this book, offered critical perspectives and friendship.

Dipak, whose work on Bundeli opened newer things.

Deepak, for always being there and for his help with indexing.

Grace, whose intellectual and emotional support comes in different forms, at times even masked in swears.

Neha Ayub, for the beautiful, apt cover page design and for what she is.

Amrith Lal, for seeing worth in every article I wrote on language.

Badminton and my circle of badminton friends—for keeping me happy and sane (and I would like to think, fit).

To my editors at OUP, especially Natasha and Darshana. To Meghali for her thoughtful professionalism and for bearing with my clumsiness. For Praveena and her team at Newgen—thank you for making this possible.

To Kodava readers and speakers—limited in number but their engagement with my work makes it worthwhile.

My family—Shubha, Kalappa, Vivek, Gangaa, Roopa, Pramod, and all the kids—for loving, for agreeing, for disagreeing. My father, for never giving up on me. My mother—to the teacher she was, to the person she was—she deserved a longer life. Muths and Poovi—who can ask for more? Nandu—for every critique you have offered, for convincing me that every idea is worth—cheers and love.

# Contents

# Introduction

## Some Thoughts on Many Aspects Around Language

Studies on languages often assume seemingly boundary-less interactions and continuities among languages of India during the precolonial period. From Bernard Cohn (1986) to Sumathi Ramaswamy (1997), from Lisa Mitchell (2009) to Nishaant Choksi (2018) and Madhumita Sengupta (2017), who albeit differ in their approaches and perceptions, have argued how languages acquired specific identities and functions during colonial times. This was aided by the writing of grammars and dictionaries, as much as administrative practices such as the census. As they have pointed out, these, with many other factors combined, have constructed languages of India in specific ways and newer linguistic and other identities are built upon these constructions.

Bernard Cohn's meticulous work argues how different forms of native knowledge systems had different specialists and noted that: 'all of these specialists were multilingual and had command of specialized languages necessary for communication between foreigners and Indians' (Cohn 1986, 277). Lisa Mitchell furthers this argument:

> In much of the Indian subcontinent, it was not unusual for literary production, pedagogy, government business and everyday communication all to take place in multiple languages. Unlike today, however, one was not expected to be able to do everything in every language in order to claim competency. Instead, individual languages typically took on specialized roles. (Mitchell 2009, 10)

While this is largely true for languages that were accepted to have specialized roles in precolonial times, as in Telugu for classical music, Telugu and Urdu in marketplaces, Persian in the court, and so on in the Deccan

*Languages of Minority.* Sowmya Dechamma CC, Oxford University Press. © Oxford University Press 2024.
DOI: 10.1093/oso/9780198908456.003.0001

region for example, the questions for us are: how and why languages like Gondi, Kodava, Yerava, Chenchu, Badaga, Toda, and many others figure in roles that hardly ever had a public/institutional presence? What specialized role did such languages perform? Why do languages of minorities remain largely in the private domain, their specific role being the domain of the private home and at best within the community? More importantly, could everyone learn what is known as classical music in Telugu? Could anyone perform the duties of an accountant conducted in a specific language, depending on the court language and the dominant language of the region? What circumscribed these roles that languages played? These roles and the people who performed these roles with specific languages were also marked by caste and the privileged positions they held in the society. Sudipta Kaviraj writes how one language in itself functions differently when used by different people, they do not belong to the language and the language does not belong to them in the same way as it does with others:

> The bhadralok of Calcutta speak the Bengali standard language, one which has resemblances on one side with the 'high' language in which Tagore wrote his poetry, but also, on the other side of the cultural spectrum, with the language spoken in the bazaar by the fisherman, the maid in the babu household, or by criminals on the margins of urban Calcutta. (Kaviraj: 2010, 128)

In addition, in most accounts of the study of languages, there is also an implicit celebration of multilinguality as a defining characteristic of precolonial India. This is also an aspect that requires our attention not just because it adds to the orientalist notions of a precolonial multilingual subcontinent that was a language paradise or language disorder[1] depending on how we see it, but also because it does not question who exactly can be or is forced to be multilingual. Even while most colonizers (not all, as Chapter One will argue) and their apparatus saw the many languages of India as chaotic, illegible, and required to be controlled through

---

[1] Karin Littau (2000) in her illuminating article 'Pandora's Tongues', brings out an interesting critique of how Derrida's understanding of linguistic chaos that he theorizes from the Tower of Babel is not just limiting the many meanings of the language that context provides us with, but also how translation can enable feminist thought and practice within the multiple interpretative meanings possible in the linguistic 'chaos'.

knowledge-producing mechanisms, postcolonial scholars of all hues have mostly seen precolonial India as a language paradise, which reaffirms certain orientalist ideologies and adds to nationalist myths.

In her introduction to *The Multilingual Nation* (2017a), Rita Kothari points to how 'India did not see an oxymoronic relationship in a "multilingual nation"—the question was identifying the right symbols that did not take away the pluralistic idea of language' (Kothari 2017a, 3). This notion of a multilingual nation serves an idea of nationhood that is pitted against a presumed monolingual European nation (an assumption that has long been contested, pointing to diverse and inequal language–society equations in European countries),[2] but also elides powerful nationalist moves towards 'one India, one language'. In the same volume, Madhumita Sengupta elaborates on how the 'sheer instability of political boundaries in the precolonial period allowed people far greater mobility that made for a higher degree of continuity in the cultural domains of geographically proximate territories (Sengupta 2017, 193)'. This as she argues, points to the disorderly and interconnected premodern universe, disorderly in contradiction to the aspiration for a presumed neat, controlled order of the colonial. In a slightly different vein, Madhava Prasad argues that the Indian case is a 'case of unfreedom arising from a linguistic disorder. And that this language disorder began with the introduction of English (93)'. "The linguistic order that has come to prevail in India is designed to perpetuate the colonial duality, to maintain a dirigiste stratum in relative insulation from the rest of the society (Prasad 2014, 95)'. While it is indeed acceptable that there were newer forms of disorders and unfreedoms with the introduction of English, the claim that the linguistic disorder began with English seems to override the disorderliness of Sanskrit, Arabic, and Persian in addition to other languages of power and court. This order imposed retrospectively on the precolonial world, linguistic or otherwise, begs the question.

That this disorderliness is not a contemporary anarchist's notion of free life, that this interconnected geographies and lives was definitely part of other premodern universes, where monarchies and caste–gender dictums worked side by side to produce histories of particular kinds are issues that go unaddressed.

[2] See, for example, Michael Cronin (2009) and Alexandra Jaffe (2009).

Indeed, language as a category was used by Europeans to construct an idea of India in a manner now famously known as orientalist in which the language and its speakers became objects of knowledge aiding the British rulers in their control of the colony in more ways than one. Obviously, this transformed the ways in which people were classified and grouped in Indian society. As Cohn observed:

> the vast social world that was India had to be classified, categorized, and bounded before it could be hierarchized [ ... ] The discursive formation was to participate in the creation and reification of social groups with their varied interests. It was to establish and regularize a discourse of differentiations which came to mark the social and political map of nineteenth-century India. (Cohn 1985, 283–284)

The problem this study attempts to explore is located in the gaps of already existing hierarchies that colonial modes only brought to fore. More importantly, my effort is to see how colonial modes enabled languages that until then functioned only within the domain of smaller communities, within privatespheres. What interests me is how certain colonial modes made these languages visible in the public by institutionalizing them through their documentation and study. I explore how colonialism introduced English—a language of power and knowledge but yet accessible to all unlike Sanskrit/Persian—thereby enabling their speakers access into different forms of knowledge. In addition, what concerns this study is how differently did these forms of knowledge constructed by nineteenth-century Europeans in these 'small' languages and in English paint ethnolinguistic minorities and what implications these have had for the people who spoke these languages.

In fact, it is extremely difficult to address these questions in modes that differ from evidence-based research. What I attempt in this work is a critique of orientalist, nationalist, and postcolonial thought that overlaps at many junctures, especially in their methods of understanding language constructs and in their methods of analysing identities and histories using these language constructs. As outlined above, these paradigms, despite their differences in approach, have largely claimed colonialism as classifying and consolidating illegible identities. These critiques of colonial knowledge formations have posited values in the precolonial uses and functions of languages and connected knowledge systems. Who can lay claim to these precolonial knowledge systems? Where exactly can we locate multilingual forms of knowledge? How are these made available to us in academia or to others?

## The Who and What of Being Multilingual

In the 2019 book *Multilingualism and the Literary Cultures of India*, published by Sahitya Akademi,[3] almost all the articles maintain a reverence to multilinguality, whether it is K. Satchidanandan, or Jasbir Jain, or Amiya Dev. Amiya Dev writes how 'Inter-Indian bilingualism is said to have thrived during medieval times. But in modern times we cannot think of much' (Dev 2019, 5). For Satchidanandan, we have lived comfortably with many languages and he finds 'this diversity extremely productive in cultural terms. [ … ] the idea of mono-lingual (also mono-religious and mono-cultural) society having come from the West' (Satchidanandan 2019, 64–65). In the same volume Harish Tridevi's probing question 'who or what is multilingual', provides us with insights that challenge the much romanticized notion of multilingualism in India.

> When we say India is a multilingual country, do we mean that the people living in the country are multilingual, or that even if most of them are monolingual as individuals, the country on the whole is multilingual and thus greater than the sum of its parts? (Tridevi 2019, 50)

Tharakeshwar carries forward Trivedi's observations and argues how institutions in independent India, especially academic literary studies based in university departments and in institutions like Sahitya Akademi, are based on a single language and this itself 'is a product of linguistic nationalism', and this points towards monolingualism and not multilingualism.

Using data from the Government of India census, Trivedi argues that it is the latter—that most Indians are monolingual—a fact that census data from 2011 is very clear about.[4] Further, Trivedi points to how we cannot

---

[3] Sahitya Akademi is the central government-run academy of of letters.
[4] https://language.census.gov.in/showDashboard

really take into consideration the small section of elite in academia who are more likely to be bi/multilingual, a context that is similar to the elite of the monarchic court who were likely the only multilinguals. This as Trivedi writes is an exception rather than the rule. Note that in contemporary India: 'the rate of bilingualism is comparatively high among the speakers of non-scheduled languages' (S. S. Bhattacharya 2002, 59), thus making it clear that it is indeed the speakers of minority languages who speak (not write) many languages, likely out of necessity.

> A recent study suggested that a substantial number of Indians speaking various languages are mostly geographically segregated; that is, the linguistic states representing the scheduled languages are becoming increasingly homogeneous. The study adds that Indian cosmopolitanism is higher in its cities than its villages, confirming [ … ] that border districts with multiple languages are being increasingly forced into the state language. Indeed, in an earlier study, it was found that Kerala was India's least linguistically diverse state as of 2011, with 97% of the state's population recognising Malayalam as their mother tongue.[5]

There is also another way in which one can understand multilingualism—the variations within a single language at the level of the individual and at the societal level which Agnihotri rightfully terms as multilingualism. Citing his own example and examples from various studies and also the often-cited differences/similarities between Hindi, Urdu, and Hindustani, Agnihotri argues how most languages would not fit into the 'linguist's or policy maker's idea of "a language". They (languages) are highly fluid, constantly being code-mixed and code-switched with each other and often moving along a trajectory that had some homogeneity at the one end and an enormous heterogeneity on the other' (Agnihotri 2022, 290). That these changes can be observed within a language in its usage by each individual and also at various stratums of society (the formalized, standardized version of the language and the one spoken at home/market being one of the many examples) makes our understanding of multilingualism

---

[5] Shashidhar, Karthik (2018): 'Nagaland Is the Most Diverse State In India, Language-Wise', *Livemint*, 11 July, https://www.livemint.com/Politics/N5QQIaSOB5GVUMP0IM3f6K/Nagaland-is-the-most-diverse-state-in-India-language-wise.html. Accessed 27 August 2020.

complex. In this understanding, multilingualism indicates the very 'fluid multilingual competence and behaviour' (Agnihotri 2022, 299).

Agnihotri also notes how the powerful languages have a bearing on the not-so-powerful languages. This is something that M. B. Emeneau observed in the early twentieth century and is found in the recent census observations, that multilinguality functions at two ends of the societal spectrum,[6] one belonging to the very learned and elite group for whom acquiring languages (associated with power) increases their social and financial capital, and at the other end, the speakers of languages of minorities and ethnolinguistic minorities who cannot function in a sphere outside their linguistic boundary/home without acquiring the dominant language of the region. In his study of the communities belonging to Nilgiri Hills of Tamil Nadu, Emeneau observes that:

> communication between Todas and Badagas involved bilingualism for the Todas rather than for the Badagas [ ... ]. How many Badagas reciprocated by learning Toda is unknown, [ ... ]. Considering the low status of the Kotas, I would guess that the Todas spoke in Toda, and the Kotas had to do the hard work of understanding—in other words, such bilingualism as there was devolved on the Kotas. In situations involving Badagas and Kotas, it seems probable that the Kotas were forced to be bilingual. (Emeneau 1994a, 391)

Thus, we see that it is people who inhabit the geopolitical cusps, ethnolinguistic minorities and other minorities who for reasons of survival will have to learn the dominant language of the region, will have to learn the 'public'/institutional language. It is these people who are likely to be multilingual while the speakers of dominant languages have no reason to learn other languages precisely because of the pervasive and dominant presence of their language. In the context of south Karnataka, the expectation will always be on a Kodava speaker to know Kannada, or for a Yerava speaker to know Kodava or in the context of Bengal, for a Ho speaker to know Bangla and never the other way around.

---

[6] https://timesofindia.indiatimes.com/india/indias-most-and-least-tongue-tied-communit ies/articleshow/66600187.cms

In the context of Yerava, Kodava and Malayalam, Mallikarjun points out how

> Kodava uses a mix of Kodava and Yerava, especially when a Kodava speaks to a Yerava. A Yerava speaks to a Kodava in Kodava. The shops, hotels and other business establishments around Yeravas are run by Malayalee Mapillas. Because of mutual dependence, the Yeravas and Malayalam speakers understand each other's language to the extent that the transaction demands such an understanding. (Mallikarjun 1993, 49–50)

What this shows is that multilingualism among lesser known (and 'lesser') communities is a matter of survival. And as can be observed, it is usually the person lowered in the social hierarchy who has to learn the relatively more privileged person's language as in when a Yerava speaks to Kodava in Kodava or a Kodava speaks to a Kannada speaker in Kannada. To these I can add many examples where people expect Tulu speakers in Hyderabad to be well versed in Kannada just because the Tulu region is officialized within the Karnataka state. That the Tulu speaker might be well versed in Tulu, English, Telugu, and Urdu and that the Kannada speaker might just know Kannada, a Hindi speaker just Hindi, and English hardly matters. Multilingualism therefore holds a mirror to the whole network of power that operates within our society. This is a point that most valorizations of multilinguality in India miss. As pointed out, studies from various theoretical and political positions have foregrounded this multilingual nature of India. The obvious difference between many languages spoken in a given region and most people of the region being able to speak more than one language seems to be lost. Also lost is the crucial point that it is only at the extreme ends of societal hierarchy that multilingualism operates.

Observations from other parts of India provide us with another perspective on the idea of multilingualism. 'Chotanagpur, Jharkhand is the only area in the entire country where three major cultural streams—Aryan, Dravidian, and Austroasian—represented through various languages have converged' (Khubchandani 2002, 99). Uttarakhand and Himachal in the northern part of India have numerous speakers of Pahari languages. 'Whether tribal and non-tribal, these communities are characterised by subaltern identities, distinct from the mainstream Hindi' (Khubchandani 2002, 99). That these groups of people with distinct but subaltern identities, stratified by various categories from within, are bilingual in Hindi and are often subsumed under the dominant communitarian identity of Hindi/Bengali/Odiya further complicates our idea of multilingualism.

Kodagu in Karnataka, a region with numerous other regions within it, offers layers of power often played through politics of communities. The Kembatti Holeya community for example, 'is known to have no other language/dialect of its own except the Kodava language. Other communities in Kodagu have a home language of their own. Kodava language, none the less, becomes their mother tongue because as (former) slaves, they are but orphans' (Somayyaji 2011, 144).

What is troubling is the narrative of a seamless and smooth transition between these layers of identities. In what ways is a consensus built around the regional identity and the national identity? How are the demarcations between ancestral, regional, and national made so clear? What powers are at play at the ancestral, local, regional, and national levels? How does Santali as a locally dominant language and community engage with 'lesser' language and communities? What is the relationship between the speakers of Santali and speakers of Hindi/Bengali/Odia? What is the relationship between speakers of Santali and speakers of Ho, Munda, and Kurukh? For example, consider Murmu's observations: 'Santali is spoken not only by about one crore Santals of the country, it is also spoken by the Ho, Munda, and Mahali Tribes of India because of their living together and because of some degree of mutual intelligibility due to language contacts' (Murmu 2002, 242). We see how the layers of hierarchical structures operate here crisscrossing notions of multilingualism and lived lives of communities. And, there is no indication if Santali speakers are familiar with Ho, Munda, and Mahali.

Emeneau's observations in the 1930s charted the manner in which languages learned and spoken by communities in a particular region like Nilgiris is heavily inflected by the hierarchies that operate between the communities and how multilingualism is a forced phenomenon on minorities. Similar examples can be found in contemporary Assam as argued by Manoranjan Pegu:

It has to be noted that most tribal communities speak Assamese but return their own respective languages as their mother tongues. For example, in the Mising Tribe, which I belong to, a large majority speak
Assamese. This is not because of school education, but mainly because
of the fact that Assamese is the dominant market language, at least in
the Brahmaputra Valley. (Pegu 2020, 6)

Though Pegu does not put it in words, the implication is clear—that
you will hardly find a speaker claiming Assamese or Axomiya as their
mother tongue to know the languages Mising or Karbi or Tiwas or Rabha.
The burden of nationalisms, however one defines it, is on the minority.
If Kodava in relation to Kannada is expected to fulfil Kannada nationalist responsibilities in a structure wherein Kodava's position is definitely
lower, in relation to Yerava, Kuruba, Kapala, and other languages/com-
munities, it is Kodava that takes the position of the oppressor.

While Pattabhirama Somayyaji, quoted above, hits the nail on the
head, the problem is that he sees this phenomenon only with the lens of
colonialist desire of the Kodava. However, the Kodagu region also poses
a problem to a linear understanding of caste and community structures
with Kodavas being outside caste and being closer to 'colonial' desires.[7]
It is precisely this desire that has propelled the Kodava into a 'modern'
sphere that is so undesirable to the caste eye that is the subject of another
chapter. As Bodisattva Kar so aptly puts it, the relationship between language and communities lends a template that always infinitely repro-
duces hierarchies (Kar 2008, 50).

While questioning the foregrounding of writing in the making of history, Prathama Banerjee notes how the language scenario amongst the
multilingual spaces connecting Adivasis and non-Adivasis have been
monolingualized during colonial and nationalist times.

Even early colonisers could not but note constant activities of translation and interpretation in the area across registers of Sanskrit, Persian,
Hindustani, several variants of Tibetan language as well as 'Parbuttia,

---

[7] This is a term used by Pattabhirama Somayyaji and also used by many scholars to point to
how certain minorities tend towards a desire and aspiration towards English, the language and
culture of the colonizer. This rings similar to the elite nationalists critique of Ambedkar who was
seen as too 'modern' and not as nationalist as the privileged caste nationalist elites.

Lepcha, Bhotea, Limboo and the Mech'. This multilingual scene was eventually unraveled, through missionary printing presses and nationalist intellectual labour, into the distinct monolingual spaces of Assam and Bengal. (Banerjee 2016, 148)

What is significant in Banerjee's observation is that it accounts for the role of the nationalist intellectuals alongside colonizer–administrator and missionary in the transformation of the assumed precolonial multilingual space into monolingual one. But the question that goes unaddressed is what kind of movement was possible for Lepcha, Bhotea, Limboo, and Mech in relation to Sanskrit and Persian, how have Lepcha, Bhotea, Limboo, and Mech made their forays into Sanskrit and Persian in ways other than being appropriated? In addition, translation from 'smaller' to larger linguistic spaces in precolonial India and also at all times can be seen as enabling a monolingual space, as argued by Trivedi and Tharakeshwar in *Multilingualism and the Literary Cultures of India* (2019).

Arguing for a position that always saw shared languages as central to the cultural scenario of India, Orsini points out that the rootedness of languages, their connection to particular communities are very modern in nature suggesting that the multilingual landscape has always allowed for a fluid identity. 'Modern language ideologies firmly believe that languages "belong' to specific communities, be they ethnic, regional, or religious. These imagined communities get simultaneously projected into the past, present, and the future' (Orsini 2017, 50), thereby illustrating how a multilingual sphere is monolingualized. This perhaps is true for newly constituted linguistic identities during the linguistic reorganization of states in India. But if this sense of belonging is only understood as 'modern', how do we understand the belongingness of Adivasis or ethnolinguistic minorities with the lands they inhabit? Have not particular languages and particular people belonged to particular locales they have inhabited for long?

In his illuminating 1999 essay, Virginius Xaxa argues that the 'the main concern of post-colonial ethnography has been to show a close interaction between the Tribes and larger society/civilization' (1520), a post-colonial anxiety that aims at showing how identities that were unbounded were bounded by apparatuses of colonialism. Subverting these postcolonial readings, XaXa further urges us to think of tribes as self-contained communities who are bounded by spatial, cultural, and linguistic boundaries. He points out that as communities they are outside the Hindu caste fold even as signs of Hinduization exist, differentiating the caste fold from the process of Hinduization. What is also significant for us is that he suggests we use:

> [ ... ] the term of reference for the study of Tribes in India [should depend on] the terms that tribal people themselves use to identify themselves and as they are identified by the people in adjacent habitations. It is common experience that groups and communities brought under the broad category of Tribe generally see say, as Santhals, Oraons, Khasis or Garos and not as Tribesmen. (XaXa 1999, 1524)

It then becomes obvious from the above and from a general observation that these indigenous people, and the names they are known by, the communities they belong to, are also the names of the languages they speak. The name of the community and name of their language share the same term with the land they inhabit. Anvita Abbi's observation that indigenous or tribal or Adivasi people (I have used these terms interchangeably) 'have reaffirmed their allegiance to their "tongue", correctly recognizing their language as the basic mark of their identity as a people' (1997. 5). So then, we have the Khasi language belonging to Khasi people in the Khasi hills; Yerava language to Yerava people in the borders of what is now Karnataka and Kerala; Bodo people speaking the Bodo language belonging to the Bodo Hills; Kodava people speaking the Kodava language inhabiting Kodagu; and so on. Khasis, Yeravas, Gonds, Kodavas, Badagas, and many such communities identify themselves with a clear notion of a region, territory, language, culture, which makes easier our task of distinguishing them as ethnolinguistic minorities. This does not hold true for 'larger' speech communities, who more often than not, are characterized by caste or their religious affiliation. Since larger speech communities are so divided by caste that is absent in the Adivasi systems, Ambedkar argued for an overarching linguistic identity that can at least attempt to overcome caste divisions. This also makes clear how dominant languages and dominant imagined communities are made of power, of nation state, that assume an all-encompassing nature, thereby subsuming 'actual' language communities that are rooted in specific locales often at the peripheries of power as Banerjee's work shows us.

> We know that modern history came to be based in India on what we now call State Archives and State Sahitya Parishads, which were largely mono-lingual collections of documents and books located in the vernacular regions—eventually to become linguistic states of the Indian Union. So we have Bengali history, Assamese history, Marathi history, Oriya history and so on. In this division of historical specialization, Adivasi language materials do not quite constitute a recognizable archive. (Banerjee 2016, 48–149)

The problem Banerjee points to is the historical conditions that have made Adivasi languages unqualified to enter the club of literary vernaculars. As discussed above, my concern is how this historicity that disqualifies languages of minorities cannot just be located in the 'modern' colonial and nationalist context, but has to be seen in its complex engagement with language communities that exist side by side and also in their aspiration and workings with English. While Dalit communities have to some extent been successful in creating a vernacular and also an English-based history and mobility, Adivasi identities that are culturally, politically, and linguistically different from that of caste communities require a methodology through which dominant tools of history, literature, and ideologies can be challenged. I think working with languages is a good place to begin with. This definitely cannot be done by merely positing the precolonial space as a multilingual one. One must also constantly ask 'who exactly was/is multilingual', and this question can better enable us to explore the relationships between people who spoke different tongues, multiple tongues, and tongues that did not require the script, at least until recently.

## 'Writing' Histories

Multilinguality is only one of the categories used to categorize ethno-linguistic minorities and cannot be generalized as a phenomenon encompassing the whole of India. Very shaky terrains of questions related to orality, script, notions of mother tongue, distinctions made between language and dialect, questions associated with literary history (or lack of it), associations between a language, race, and people, are categories with which minoritized languages are strongly associated. This work attempts to address: how scholars of various hues have used these categories to talk about a people; how this points to an understanding that complicates heretofore held notions of orientalist representation; how studies on languages of India, including by scholars of Indian origin, have largely been on major languages whose aspirations and contexts vastly differ from most languages in India. Briefly, my concern is to attempt a critique of how orientalism and postcolonial thought have largely claimed colonialism as heralding undesirable identities that classify languages and people in fixed categories. Although not directly, these critiques of colonial knowledge formations have posited values in the precolonial functions of language and related knowledge systems of a society deeply entrenched in casteist patriarchies. Despite Prathama Banerjee urging us to think about 'how such a field compels us to rethink our relationship with text, archive and field, that is, the evidentiary paradigm that grounds social science today' (Banerjee 2016, 131), studies thus far have largely focused on histories of languages that had a written record, the focus being on 'writing' as the primary text used for analysis, 'writing' as the reliable evidence—a methodology that has often gone unquestioned even as critiques of positivist empiricism have become common place.

In the very same essay, Banerjee moves on to argue how Adivasis are not seen as embodiments of past histories precisely because neither a written literature nor institutionalized religion was central to their histories, and therefore ethnography became a convenient method for non-Adivasis to construct Adivasi lives (note, not histories). Although there has been considerable work on oral histories, it is marked as a separate domain away from the boundaries of history proper. History proper and its methods do not consider our utterances and representations, in effect part of oralities. Hayden White (1992), one of the most influential historians of our times has successfully argued for history as a narrative, as a form of storytelling. His observation that history has always privileged the act of writing is very crucial to our own understanding of history in relation to orality. As Tyler Stovall argues:

[N]one of the historians of historiography that I knew had taken seriously the fact that historiography was first, necessarily, and most obviously *writing*, which is to say, inscription, of words or signs incised or
laid upon a medium and which, by that process of inscription, are endowed with a power both material and spiritual, a power to at once 'fix'
things in time and seemingly reveal their meaning for their own time
and for our own.[8]

Even as Joan Scott accounts for the advantages of considering experience as evidence in historiography, she cautions us about how experience
has to lead us to 'exploring how difference is established, how it operates, how and in what ways it constitutes subjects who see and act in the
world' (Scott 2009, 777). This is significant for us because one cannot just
posit orality as difference but we will have to look into how orality is construed as difference and how it functions as a category within history and
the multiple uses history and literary history are engaged in. In Urvashi
Butalia's words:

Oral history is a methodological tool that many feminist historians
have found enormously empowering. Looking at women's narratives
and testimonies, and placing them alongside, or indeed against, the official discourses of history, has offered feminist historians a new and
different way of looking at history. (Butalia 2000, 16)

For Ranjit Guha attempting to address the question of who decides what
is history and 'to what values and criteria' underpin history, it is only too
obvious that history is nominated so by 'none other than an ideology
for which the life of the state is all there is to history' (Guha 1996, 1).
Therefore, in what Guha calls statism lies the authority to determine what
constitutes history implying that history is nothing but what and how the
state desires to represent its power and culture. The problem with Guha's
'The small voice of history' is that the connection between history and
state is established as almost exclusively European, and how this institution of history entered South Asia via colonialism. Not only does this

---

[8] https://www.historians.org/publications-and-directories/perspectives-on-history/septem
ber-2018/hayden-v-white-(1928%E2%80%932018). Accessed 9 November 2020.

essentialize Europe's history as one that is characterized only by bourgeoisie concerns thereby excluding the small voices from European history but also sidelines the connection between history and political power in precolonial South Asia. How do we understand precolonial South Asian history and what constitutes it? This question becomes interesting when Pollock inserts the aesthetics of language in the representation of political culture in South Asia. For Pollock, history and its representation of political culture, available mainly through literary cultures (written) and inscriptions is ample evidence of how historical representation is inseparably connected to the political power in South Asia and that this power is manifested via the elevation of writing and incorporating writing in particular aestheticized forms. What is significant in Pollock's work is the centrality assigned to language, writing, and aesthetics in unravelling the relationship between historiography and political culture. Albeit Guha's focus on the history of women's struggles in the Telangana movement in the late 1940s and on how these small voices can challenge statist discourses, how they bring back agency and instrumentality of various actors in history, how it leads the way for other small voices to be heard, and how it interrupts the dominant version thereby making history itself disorderly and stutter (11–12); what does not assume centrality in Guha's 'small voice' is that it is a voice to be *heard*, it is an oral narrative to be listened to with utmost care even as it interrupts, unlike the often written/inscribed statist discourse.

In the same volume of *Subaltern Studies* that Guha poses this connection between statism and historiography, Ajay Skaria carries this relationship further to bring in the act of writing as one that is crucial to colonial power but nevertheless vulnerable to various other powers including that of orality. But Skaria, too, sees the power of writing (and that of state history) as being overridden by European bourgeoisie ideologies. In what he terms as a myth around writing—the magical nature of writing—the myth model 'was made possible of course, by the assumption that literacy was characteristic of 'civilized' societies' (Skaria 1996, 16) and made commonsensical by colonial domination and by European scholars, Skaria's attempt is to show how colonizers perpetuated this myth. This myth model as Skaria, quoting De Certeau, rightly points out, epitomizes learning, civilization, and all that distinguishes the West from the Rest (Skaria 1996, 51).

The 'oral' is that which does not contribute to progress; reciprocally, the 'scriptural' is that which separates itself out from the magical world of voices and traditions. A frontier (and a front) of Western culture is established by that separation. Thus one can read above the portals of modernity such inscriptions as 'Here, to work is to write', or 'Here, only what is written is understood'. (quoted in Skaria 1996, 51)

Skaria goes on to note how 'This formula—writing equals modernity—is in part the consequence of its historical role in the consolidation of state power and domination' (Skaria 1996, 51). What Sheldon Pollock has made us aware of is this—the power of writing, the written word's connection to dominant knowledge, and to the dominant ritual and political power for at least the last 2000 years in India, prior to colonialism. Unlike Skaria, Guha, or Banerjee, Pollock's study does not limit the relationship between power, writing, and civilization to Europe but extends this connection to the precolonial South Asian context as well.

For Skaria, this persuasive nature of writing is further compounded by a fetishization of writing (51). Using Jack Goody, Walter J. Ong, and others, Skaria notes how this continued fetish for writing becomes exemplary with anthropology and history that saw the 'savage' as the epitome of speech whose 'other' was the civilized being (16). We will see how precisely these and other categories that discredit orality become agential in James Scott. But Skaria's task lies in developing a framework that 'avoids both the reification of the distinction between orality and literacy, and the historical closure of the argument with the valid but limited point that the meanings of writing varied in different contexts' (18). Skaria's reference to writing being used as a 'powerful plains technology' is in parenthesis, and possibly earlier than the nineteenth century, where Dangis saw writing as a tool of power of people from plains (18). Quoting Mudimbe, Skaria argues against an epistemological ethnocentrism that presumes a valorization of writing among the 'non-literate societies must necessarily be a consequence of incomprehension and wonderment in the face of an external stimulus' (30). Moreover, although Skaria mentions documentation by Mughal and Maratha regimes, the power of writing has to be seen as circumscribed by the political state, be it South Asian or colonial. And for Skaria, the interpretative community that is constituted around colonialism is 'not an aesthetic or mildly social act' (38), but an act that asserts political domination. What makes the consolidation of power via writing so very colonial? Indeed, how the aesthetics of writing is built into political domination is what Pollock shows us. How does the power of writing operate in the ritual, cultural realm? How and why has writing within South Asian communities been restricted to miniscule caste-based elites, especially men, until recently? How does it function in the realm of knowledge production including history, in the day-to-day lives of most people whose knowledge and livelihood systems did not require writing, are questions that become difficult to answer.

The above questions and also how writing in South Asia is heavily associated with the caste-based system of knowledge and politics do not figure in much of the scholarship framed by the postcolonial and/or subaltern studies. And the production and continuation of knowledge in most societies, hills, forests, or plains involved not writing but oral modes is something that is rarely addressed and which Skaria acknowledges. 'For ordinary Bhils or Koknis, literacy was almost never required [ ... ]. Rights to hunting, fishing, foraging, shifting cultivation, or land revenue were organized not by written documents but around popular oral knowledge of territorial authority' (Skaria 21).

If Guha's connection is limited by its assumption of connection between state power and history to the European bourgeoisie, Skaria limits the connection of the power of writing to the very same actors in European history. In what is one of the most illuminating studies on languages and inequalities in Europe, Baumann and Briggs meticulously explore how Europe's modernity is built on language ideologies that emerge from and create new political and social inequalities. With the coming of print, they argue, 'the transposition of word, then, from speaking to print, was assimilated to the great divide between past and present, and it has remained central to modernizing understandings to this day' (Baumann and Briggs 2003, 12). But this process of modernization in Europe has had its own 'other' wherein 'oral tradition became the foundation of a poetic of otherness, a means of identifying the premodern others both within modern society (uneducated, rural, poor, female) and outside it (savage, primitive, "pre-literate')' (Baumann and Briggs 2003,12). Provincializing Europe is what Baumann and Briggs essentially do while the task for us is to provincialize precolonial South Asia, desacralize the written/scriptural word, provincialize historiography and its changing relationship to power, both gendered and casteist, within India. This is a task still un-accomplished which historians like Sanal Mohan are pushing us towards:

> Historical knowledge is perceived sometimes as embodiment of 'true' knowledge of the past without considering the process by which the particular knowledge of the past is created. [ ... ] Equally significant is the situatedness of knowledge production that problematizes the very theoretical assumptions behind particular interpretations. (Mohan 2015, 272)

Although Brahminical knowledge was exclusively oral until a certain point in history[9], it took refuge in writing in particular language(s) as Pollock shows us, and reinforced existing hegemonies that strategically took on various means to sustain itself. Following Tyler Williams, writing, 'is specifically inscription, the commitment of speech to writing, the transcription of oral/aural utterances into graphic sign. Accordingly, 'literacy' [ ... ] refers specifically to graphic literacy, the ability to read written language' (2018, 84). In his attempt to explore the relationship between inscription and textual composition in precolonial South Asian imagination, Williams points out that inscription (writing) was largely considered a technical skill whereas acts of 'composition was understood to be an intellectual activity of the highest order' (Williams 84). Yet, as Williams further argues, both forms, that is technical and intellectual, were 'intertwined by the early modern period and written textuality had become intertwined with aspects of religious ritual as well as literature' (84). This is something Pollock elaborates in detail via the categories of panegyric, *prasasti*, and *kavya*. Although I find it difficult to map Williams' division of technical and intellectual categories onto a premodern world, this idea comes up again in the work of Yuval Harari. Harari points out how writing/early inscription was indeed a tool of convenience as groups of *Homo sapiens* grew larger in number under some or the other form of state control and accounts needed to be maintained in ways other than memory. This led to the emergence of inscriptions that over the years came to be used to control larger and larger groups under the umbrellas of religion and state (Harari 2015, 138–148).

---

[9] Refer to Mackenzie Brown (1986).

Many researchers suggest that the use of writing in India dates back to between 2550 and 1900 BC during the Harappan civilization in which certain groups of people were definitely literate and urbane (P. G. Patel 1996; Parpola 1994; Tony Joseph 2018; Harari 2015). The people who came later, the Rigvedic people, were pastoral and and had an oral tradition. Being pastoral they needed to pass on the knowledge they held while moving constantly. It was the material practice of being in the here and now. These oral songs seem to have heavily influenced the metre and rhythm of early poetic verses, which aided in memorizing them. How does this orality, in fact an antipathy to written word in old Brahminic traditions change into a reverence for the written word is a question that Mackenzie Brown asks. Although languages have been oral since the times *Homo sapiens* used speech and writing was only a tool used by administrators and rulers for documenting, for purposes of recording revenue and for theological purposes, writing in the recent history of humans has replaced the revered place orality held, especially in South Asia after the ascendancy of Brahminic culture, after the decline of Harappan civilization. In the present day, the word is mostly if not always, often understood as the scripted word or the printed one. It is an image, fixed with the scripture. Today, the valued word is hardly ever the spoken word—it is the written word that is considered permanent. This is also so because for many, the written word was initially made accessible by Islam and Christianity, especially to lowered castes—via sacred books in their own languages, to whom sacred written/heard was denied. It was in English, in other Indian languages, and in Arabic through which the sacred was accessible and became enduring. Also the formal 'secular' schooling system that took the written word to theoretically everyone who was thus far barred from the value-laden knowledge and writing. Oral for the pastoralists of early Brahminic traditions was revered since writing was destructible. Material used for writing while on the move was not 'permanent', it could be lost in the vagaries of a mobile life. The emphasis on *Shruti* (what is heard) and on *Smriti* (what is remembered) provides us with insights into the place that orality and memory held within Vedic religion in South Asia. This meant that before print, the book/manuscript was not central to most lives. Religion was practised in many ways and it was only after Buddhism's spread roughly after 500 BCE, that Vedic words were written down and that too only for a section of Brahmin men. And since this recitation is restricted to a particular tight-knit community, it was impossible for others to learn these practices of religion, even assuming others wanted to learn them. When this tightly guarded orality was written down, it becomes much easier to decipher, to circulate, and to destroy, to steal, than when it is closed within a guarded group in the form of orality. Writing diffuses the control in many ways. Early Brahminism therefore preferred orality—since writing was alien during those times, since writing would be difficult to control within the elite group, and since writing was perishable. If and when orality was transferred into the mode of writing, the fear of losing caste purity loomed large since the word then would have been inscribed on a manuscript, embedded in caste material practices, not entirely within the control of the 'pure' community. Winternitz points to how the priestly concern to preserve the purity of the Veda from pollution by not allowing the lowered castes to learn the sacred 'texts' was more readily accomplished if texts were not written on the page. Further, Goody points to how 'In India, oral transmission was employed not only to preserve a literate monopoly, but also because of its archaic (and to some extent intrinsic) values' (quoted in Brown 1986, 72). Essentially, orality helped Sanskrit and the religion it carried retain its purity. This also meant a teacher was essential within Brahminic traditions in order to learn through listening and watching. Sound (*shruti*) and memory (*smriti*) were prioritized over meaning. Within that kind of a context, written word would engender independent learning, thinking, questioning, interpretation, and therefore was dismissed. Aniket Jaaware has another interesting perspective on how writing was indeed well within the Brahminical traditions and how:

[ ... ] texts were always written down anyway. There is a tacit acceptance of the fallibility of human memory in the writing down. [ ... ] the business of writing down these texts—all of them—is taken up in the first place in order to stabilize, standardize, and preserve them in the assumed purity of their supposed origins. (Jaaware 2019, 119)

It was the kind of knowledge that Sanskrit held, the community that controlled this knowledge in Sanskrit, that made select orality sacrosanct, and not orality per se. Brahminic traditionalists would have been aware of thousands of oral practices around them but it was the sacredness embodied in Sanskrit that made their orality 'purer', 'better' than others until the time they could control the written script. This is perhaps why the pure sacred language died pure without ever having the chance to be passed on to larger 'impure' communities in the many 'impure' languages/vernaculars they spoke. Although not by a sudden twist in the story, but through gradual twists aided by the spread of Sanskrit, that was superordinated, superpositioned on the growth of vernacular languages, writing replaced orality as the preferred mode for knowledge production and dissemination. Indeed, the spread of different religions, the spread of print capitalism, colonialism, and formal education introduced by the colonizer made writing becomes pure knowledge replacing orality. Simultaneously this meant a reinforcement of already existing discrediting/non-recognition of oral traditions of Adivasi and of other communities. We also need to note that this growth of vernaculars was modelled on the written traditions of Sanskrit precisely because it was the bilingual elite of these vernaculars, the Brahmin men, who could access writing in their vernacular and in Sanskrit, who were the first ones (and the only ones for the longest times) to write.

## What Then Is Vernacular and Its Connection to Writing and Literacy

While Sheldon Pollock has shown us how vernaculars in South Asia grew in the realm of writing via the process he calls vernacularization, Ivan Illich, in his powerful *Vernacular Values* (1980) traces the genealogy of the vernacular. 'Vernacular is a Latin term that we use in English for the language we have acquired without paid teachers. In Rome, it was used from 500 BCE to AD 600 to designate any value that was homebred, derived from the common and that a person could protect and defend though he neither bought or sold it on the market'.[10] The term *verna*, also suggesting the word 'slave' is closely related to the Sanskrit term *varna* (the caste-based system), suggesting a relationship between 'slave system' and 'caste system' and can be understood as the languages spoken by commoners,

---

[10] Ivan Illich. http://www.davidtinapple.com/illich/1980_vernacular_values.html. Accessed 12 September 2018.

and the lowered in any hierarchy. By now, as we shall see, vernacular has moved far from this usage of slave/caste albiet retaining certain implications. Following Illich, vernacular is native, not trained, not formal, and a rooted connectedness between language and people that has not been alienated from other practices of subsistence living. Languages, it is obvious, pass through various conflicting phases in history, and are often shaped by them. This phase of being vernacular is one such and if we go by Illich's understanding, most languages of the minority even today are vernaculars. This understanding can also be mapped to James Scott's understanding of orality that at times romanticizes the value of vernacular subsistence that in today's world is difficult to sustain. While Illich makes the idea of vernacular very organic, for Sheldon Pollock vernacularization is a moment in the history of a language where it gets committed to writing. Although all languages live through (and many retain) Illich's phase, Pollock's phase has been characterized by a power that is possible only for some language communities.

How the vernaculars of Europe came to be languages that carried colonialism and capitalism to almost all over the world is what Illich traces. From the idea of Elio Antonio de Nebrija, the fifteenth-century Spanish grammarian who laid the foundations for a grammar and a language as a 'tool for conquest abroad and a weapon to suppress untutored speech at home', Illich gives us a vivid account of how the spoken vernacular came to be a 'pure' written language that required training in order to be the 'consort of empire'. In Nebrija's words: 'My illustrious queen. Whenever I ponder over the token of past that have been preserved in writing, I am forced to the very same conclusion. Language has always been the consort of the empire, and forever shall remain its mate. Together they come into being, together they grow and flower, and together they decline',[11] reminding us of Lucia Boldrini's analysis of transfer of arts via the transfer of empire, *Translatio Studii et Imperii* (Boldrini 2010, 187). For us, what Illich does is provincialize Europe much like what Baumann and Briggs do—a task that urges us to provincialize worlds around us.

Pollock's vernacularization then is a carved language, carved into writing from the spoken forms of the everyday lives of people. Who gets to

---

[11] Ivan Illich. http://www.davidtinapple.com/illich/1980_vernacular_values.html. Accessed 12 September 2018.

inscribe from which form and in what form is a foregone conclusion. For Nebrija, the spoken forms were nothing but of the wild. John Aubrey, the seventeenth-century English antiquarian is quite unabashed in declaring that 'before printing, old-wives tales were ingeniose, but the divine art of printing and gunpowder have frightened away Robin-good-fellow and the fayries' (Baumann and Briggs 2003, 12). Spoken forms were heathen, they were 'old-wives tales' and the queen's (king's) language had to be civilized/pure. One cannot miss the similarity between this Christian purity and the Brahminic purity. Illich points out that Nebrija was unaware of Panini's grammar that was roughly 1500 years older than him. For Illich, Panini's work was an 'attempt to describe a dead language, to be taught only to a few'. The ungoverned and unbound speech in which people actually live and manage their lives becomes a challenge to the state. Following James Scott, we can see how ungoverned, illegitimate, and uncontrollable languages move beyond the surveillance of the state. A language therefore had to be controlled: controlled in writing and then used to control the ruler's subjects. This is a notion that holds true not just through monarchies and feudal states in Europe, but also in South Asia and also one that has survived strongly into colonialism and nation states.

As Illich shows, in a context where much of Europe's people though conversant of the literature in their region were not conversant with reading and writing (or at times had picked it up by themselves). 'Nebrija clearly showed the way to prevent free and anarchic development of printing technology, and exactly how, to transform it into the evolving nation-states' instrument of bureaucratic control'.[12]

So then, the idea of the vernacular is transformed when put to use by the state and into writing. 'The switch from the vernacular to an officially (vernacularized) taught mother tongue is perhaps the most significant and, therefore, least researched event in the coming of a commodity-intensive society' and 'as a pillar of the nation-state'.[13] Perhaps then, we can understand this switch of the vernacular to the taught mother tongue as vernacularization, a process aided by powers that are current at a given point in time.

---

[12] Illich. http://www.davidtinapple.com/illich/1980_vernacular_values.html.
[13] Illich. http://www.davidtinapple.com/illich/1980_vernacular_values.html.

Illich further notes how the uniformity, artificial, and restricted nature of Sanskrit, Greek, and Latin combined with their religiosity, led to the demise of these languages. This is significant because it is precisely these languages' alienation from people's spoken speech forms, alienation from the orality of everyday lives that led to their death. Unfortunately, the huge gaps they created in knowledge systems and amongst people before their death continue to have their implications even to this day. Even more unfortunately, it is this very same model that the new nation states have followed that seek to create an artificial, uniform language that befits their territorial and nationalist aspirations. Of course there is a clear distinction between the functioning of the monarchies and that of the nation states. If the older languages of power and religion were restricted only to the elites, the nation state imposes its uniformity; expects all its subjects to be familiar and fall in line with the uniformity of the language and associated ideology (even if everyone is not conversant in the language of power). It is only too obvious that the huge majority of the people whose worlds are a complicated negotiation between many tongues and many ideologies will hardly be able to attain the perfect uniformity that a nation aspires to. It is also obvious that the new elites of the nation state which D. L. Sheth and Paul Brass characterize as the vernacular elite/bilingual elite, capitalize on this imperfect uniformity arising out of the gaps between lived worlds and the aspirations of the nation thereby consolidating their political cultural power that is always already bequeathed to them via caste and gendered privileges.

On the other hand, S. Shankar in his *Flesh and Fish Blood: Postcolonialism, Translation, and the Vernacular* characterizes vernacular thus: 'by vernacular knowledges I mean those oriented away from the transnational, the modern, and the hybrid and toward the local, the traditional, and the culturally autonomous' (2012, xv). I would like to posit that the local can also be appropriated by the dominant and be circulated in another garb. Local can also travel through other means. And traditional is a category that is perhaps more applicable to the power of the cosmopolitan than to the working of the vernacular. In effect, like the vernacular, traditional is often seen in a relational mode with the cosmopolitan; traditional is also a construct against the presumed characteristics of the cosmopolitan/modern. Working on Tamil, Hindi, and English literary texts from India and attempting a critique of Casanova's *World*

*Republic of Letters*, Shankar points out that this understanding of vernacular can simultaneously hold multiple meanings which are not necessarily contradictory and operates in a relational mode.

> If vernacular is often opposed to classical in usage, it is also a rough synonym for local or regional. These two usages of vernacular are not in reality incompatible; they simply reveal different orientations in usage, along the axis of diachrony in one case and synchrony in the other. A classical language like Tamil, when it finds itself in the position of having to resist the transnational, might become a vernacular language. (Shankar 2012, 132)

As is evident, the usage of vernacular in recent times has moved far away from being dismissed as a denigrated term, associated with the slave. Shankar uses this term to point to the relative power that operates between languages and the manner in which they circulate via texts. While the power that languages carry via their communities is indeed the bone of contention, how this idea of vernacular works within various Tamils and what has the power of various Tamils done to the languages of minorities is a question for further probing. Like most 'regional' languages of power, Tamil being the foremost (including Malayalam, Kannada, Bangla, Hindi, and such), their cosmopolitan vernacular aspirations have only reproduced hierarchies between these dominant 'regional' languages and languages spoken by Adivasis and other linguistic minorities, making them invisible. It is here that Sheldon Pollock's idea of vernacular becomes pertinent. While discussing the process of vernacularization, he points to how:

> vernacular intellectuals define a literary culture in conscious opposition to something larger; they choose to write in a language that does not travel—and that they know does not travel—as easily as the well-traveled language of the cosmopolitan order. [ ... ] that this 'local' in turn typically comes to be constructed as dominant and dominating for smaller cultural spaces is a further step in the cosmopolitan–vernacular transformation and unthinkable without it. (Pollock 1998, 8)

In one of the recent 'provocations' on the vernacular, South Asian Review (2020, 41 (2) carried articles by four scholars working in the area. Indeed, all of them point to the inevitable that vernacular is a term that cannot but be used in relation to a 'high' language, often standardized, often the ones that travel and are cosmopolitan. What is very useful is Shankar's understanding—that 'the vernacular is one more instrument in the toolbox of critical theory. Its greatest potency and potential is when it is understood as such' (Shankar 2020, 192). Interestingly, Francesca Orsini quoting Ferguson makes a connection between multilingual and vernacular and prefers the theoretical category of multilingual to vernacular. 'The word vernacular, therefore, speaks to situations of hierarchical bilingualism (called diglossia), in which one or more high languages are formally taught through schools, manuals, grammars, and dictionaries, and provide access to administrative jobs and high culture' (Orsini 2020, 204). As discussed earlier in this introduction, this idea of multilingualism exists in the extreme spectrums of the society, among a miniscule elite and among people on the periphery. Further, Orsini points to how South Asia, 'despite significant regional differences—has been a multilingual situation, in which vernaculars (Hindi, Urdu, Bengali, Gujarati, Marathi, etc.) have continued to coexist with one or more high languages, and with other regional languages, with local languages, and with specialized argots and scripts' (Orsini 2020, 205). This coexistence will have to take into consideration the skewed relationship between these languages and the people who speak them. Not just hierarchies, coexistence also does not necessarily mean languages inhabit the same space, in the same manner, and that more than two languages are used by individuals. This coexistence of multilinguality often indicates the separate domains that languages and people inhabit without ever having anything to do with each other, other than being in a clear hierarchical relationship, very much like caste. So, vernacular for us, in this book, is a space that simultaneously challenges notions of coexistence while envisioning radical spaces of coexistence.

It is also pertinent that Shankar observes that language is not the only living and theoretical category that vernacular can refer to.

The vernacular as a critical term has enabled a burgeoning attention to caste. It would be wrong to posit a natural association between the vernacular and caste, any more than between the vernacular and language. Dalit voices are not to be found only in the vernacular but they are to be found differently, and more loudly, in the vernacular. (Shankar 2020, 192)

While the usage of the term vernacular in this book is definitely connected to languages of ethnolinguistic minorities and communities referred to as minorities—which include the languages and language varieties spoken by Dalits, ethnolinguistic minorities, and religious minorities—it differs from the manner in which it is conceptualized by Shankar. For, as much as vernaculars have the 'subaltern tinge' (Orsini 2020, 205), vernaculars like Tamil, Kannada, or Hindi have more often than not been used to reinforce the caste, gender, and communitarian hierarchies. It is in these powerful 'vernaculars', it is in their ability to function with multiple positions and meanings that these networks of power most efficiently circulate. The need to distinguish between the vernacular as used by the elite castes and as used by Dalits and other minorities becomes imperative, for especially in its written form vernacular is most accessible to and malleable by casteist patriarchy. Albeit Dalits have been able to use the written form of vernacular, for a large section of Dalits, the institutionalized and standardized written forms of knowledge and circulation is distant, alienating, and oppressive not to mention the many erasures.[14]

In the languages I am familiar with (other than English), this conceptual difference between a vernacular and a language is not at all clear or does not exist. In Kodava, the language I grew up in, a language is known as *takk*, meaning something that is spoken. *Takk* also means to speak. Writing is known as *Elth*, which has similarities with the Tamil and Malayalam terms for writing. The two dominant dialects of Kodava, *Kiggatt takk* and *Mendele takk*, are also known as *takk* thereby blurring the non-existent distinction between a language and dialect. All are languages in this sense. Similarly, Kannada, the language I was institutionally trained in, uses the term *maatu* both for the act of speaking and also for language. Kannada also uses the term *bhashe* to refer to language that is used in quite formal contexts and not for colloquial speech. Telugu, a language I have learned much later in life uses the terms *maata* and *bhasha*

---

[14] For how Hindi operates among Adivasis, see the illuminating article https://www.thehindu.com/features/magazine/lost-in-interpretation/article7018549.ece

in a sense similar to that in Kannada. Dipak Barkhade[15] referring to this distinction in his doctoral dissertation mentions how in dominant Hindi the distinction between standard language and spoken language is made distinct by the terms *bhasha* and *boli*, respectively. In our understanding, *boli* can be referred to as the vernacular and one that becomes *bhasha* after it goes through the process of vernacularization. G. N. Devy uses this understanding of *bhasha* as well: 'The emergence of new languages—*bhashas*—all over the Indian subcontinent [ … ] expressed regional and heterodox aspirations in protest against the hegemony of Sanskrit' (Devy 2019, 30), while simultaneously drawing upon written Sanskritized models. The understanding I want to take forward is that the process of becoming *bhasha* is close to the concept of dominant vernacularization. These *bhashas* in the process and after vernacularization, reproduce the binaries and inequalities among *takk/boli/maatu/and other* speech forms. I want to emphasize that even after a language is vernacularized, the vernacularized form is only one of the forms in which the language continues to survive, albeit this being the most powerful form. Despite being vernacularized and standardized, all languages even today mostly live in their organic vernacular forms, which are their spoken forms. As is clear, many languages have had no requirement to be vernacularized, and many languages have never been able to enter or access the sphere of vernacularization that has been within the control of religious and/or state-based institutions of power. This work therefore differentiates 'vernacular' from 'vernacularization'. I understand both as processes that function differently for different purposes and used by different kinds of people. Although some of these processes overlap as Shankar points out, what for me differentiates these two processes is the degree of power they hold and exert. Even as some of them might be going through the process of vernacularization, there is no way we can compare this with languages that are already dominantly vernacularized. Just to give an example, how can we ever compare Lotha, the language spoken by the Lothas of Nagaland now beginning to be written, vernacularized with languages like Bengali or even Assamese? I therefore draw both from Illich and from Pollock in my usage—vernacular as the term for the languages that have continued to live in orality, live in subsistence within the local economy

---

[15] Dipak Barkhade, unpublished PhD thesis. University of Hyderabad, 2022.

they are part of, that have begun to be written down recently, that have had little or no institutional support, and whose powers and functions are localized. Vernaculars then are languages that are not yet vernacular-ized, not yet there in their formal written status, not yet standardized, and therefore not imposed on other communities via a circulation made possible largely through writing and print. Vernacularized languages, in contrast, are languages that are already standardized, institutionalized, exert relative power, have official and state patronage be it the powerful English or Hindi, or Kannada, Telugu, Tamil, Bangla, and such. It is also pertinent to note that the term 'vernacularized', the verb of the noun 'vernacular' is to render the social process visible.[16] In short, I use the term vernacular for a language that is not vernacularized, was happy to be in that state, did not require to be vernacularized, and at times was not allowed to be vernacularized.

Vernaculars and their oralities/performative arts travel too—the most often used example being how *Ramayana* and *Mahabharata* have travelled and have taken various shapes and meanings. But until the coming of print, these performative texts were localized and different meanings and interpretations were also localized and accepted within the locales.[17] Dominant writing/manuscripts travelled too, in Sanskrit and in courtly vernaculars, via translations, interpretations, and via faithful copies as well. Only with the coming of print capitalism, the notion of 'original' and the authority of a text and that of the author get consolidated and even more standardized.[18] However, there is a crucial difference because these textual travels are largely one way, top down. The epics *Ramayana* and *Mahabharata* travelled only because they were powerful in more senses than one (including being manuscripted in many dominant/court languages of India and were patronized by the courts). We hardly know of epics/performative texts of ethnolinguistic minorities/Adivasis that have travelled like *Ramayana* or *Mahabharata*. Who knows the *Iggutappa*[19] story of Kodavas? Why has it not travelled like the Hindu

---

[16] This is also the principle on which my usage of 'lowered' is based in the phrase 'lowered caste', as against the commonly used phrase 'lower caste'. For more on this process where the verbing of nouns renders the social process visible, see J. R. Martin (2008). I thank Sushrut Jadhav for alerting me to this work.

[17] A. K. Ramanujan (1991) and Paula Richman (1991).

[18] Michel Foucault (1979).

[19] *Iggutappa*, the god of food to many in the Kodagu region.

epics? Essentially, these texts in Kodava or Ho that have not travelled (but have definitely changed over time and contexts) and have maintained specific relationships with speakers of the language community that are vernacular. These vernaculars like Kodava and Ho are just beginning to be vernacularized, but are home-bred and without aspirations for larger powers, albeit not without power hierarchies that are internal to their region. One also needs to note that these vernaculars have definitely changed dominant languages and their texts in very many ways but these are hardly made visible or acknowledged. The reverse traffic or movement of languages, ideas from the vernacular to the dominant vernacularized languages has been a long neglected area.

There is also a connection that I want to emphasize between the processes of vernacularization and standardization. To a large extent vernacularization of any language and the process through which it is put to literary writing involves standardization. Vernacularized languages, essentially the ones that are formalized through writing systems and in other media systems often work with boundedness of rules with regards to grammar (Le Page 2020, 95). They have a clear-cut understanding of how language has to be used, especially in the written form and in institutional usages. As an example, Le Page point to how 'by the end of the seventeenth century the written language of the intellectuals among the bourgeosie of the Ile-de-France which was seen as having reached a stage of near perfection, which was held up as a model' (Le Page 2020, 86). This is something which Bourdieu details in his *Language and Symbolic Power* (1991). As is evident, many of the languages classified as scheduled, as official, as national languages, are standardized through similar processes in different contexts. Hindi in the context of nationalism and related Hindu communal fervour associating itself with high Sanskrit, Urdu in the same time period but in a different trajectory are the ones that are most often quoted (Shamsur Faruqi, Paul Brass, Alok Rai, Christopher King). Even languages that are not classified as scheduled or official often go through processes of standardization, processes that bestow prestige to one dialect and less prestige to the other. This standardization creates complex difficulties for the not-so-standardized languages—difficulties from dominant languages notwithstanding— difficulties and interference from a standardized version of one's own language create debilitating consequences.

This finite rule-based nature of language use (which keeps changing) along with stereotypes around language usages of less powerful communities/individuals are what leads to standardization alongside print capitalism, formation of nations, and subsequent construction of national icons such as national languages, use of particular kinds of language in education, media, and related phenomena. The most widespread myth around language today perhaps is that the written language is the 'correct' or the 'standard' form of language and all spoken varieties of the same language are its variants. The fact that no language emerged in its written form—as writing evolved much later from the various forms of the spoken—is a logic that is missed by such myths. Needless to say, with a rule-boundedness, standardization is accompanied by acts of power where one particular dialect attains the status of the language and other dialects 'remain dialects'. As William Bright rightly puts it, the diversities and variations in languages are not fact free but is 'co-related with systematic social difference' and it is our task to address this (Bright 1966).

## How Then Can We Understand Orality?

'It has [also] been rather common to see oral traditions as a historical layer that preceded literature, constituting its generic system in an inchoate and primitive form' (Niklander 2018, 7). To see oral as divorced from other forms of expression is pointless because throughout known history, oral language has continuously engaged with the written.

What is more interesting to me is the point about orality and modernity that Niklander makes. 'Because of its long history of existence, oral tradition or folklore becomes a modern construct' (Niklander 8). Although a modern construct or precisely because it is a modern construct, Baumann and Briggs show that orality has been constructed in opposition to the modern. But where Baumann and Briggs differ is in the argument of inequality they bring in that has constructed orality as belonging to the 'lesser' people.

The ideological construction of modernity in terms related to print culture and its associated discursive formations is more fully and clearly explainable as part of a more comprehensive process that depended upon the construction of a contrastive past, characterised by contrasting technologies and modes of communication. (Baumann and Briggs 2003, 14)

How these contrastive constructs used language, and writing and orality as categories that marked people in contrasting inequal ways is the question Baumann and Briggs ask. One could ask many more questions around writing and orality—can writing be studied independently of orality? How do we understand the primacy posited in writing while orality is largely studied today via the written text and via recording? 'It would perhaps be self-evident that different material practices of writing give rise to, and are in turn shaped by, different ways of imagining language, memory, and knowledge' (Williams 2018, 82). Further, is writing not based on hearing and listening? Is not field-based research and its writing entirely dependent on non-written forms of representations and do we not perceive ethnographic writing itself as another representation?.

Today, while much of the oral tradition is documented in writing or recording and made accessible to the reading public, the paradox is this—orality, which was once accessible to all, is now made accessible to those who can read. In effect, it is made accessible to those who cannot and/or are not willing to listen. When I pointed out how oral transmission of songs in Kodava had almost stopped, my father, now in his eighties and has lived in Kodagu throughout his life, said something very interesting. In his view, until his childhood, there were spaces like the village common grounds and the hills where he and his friends took cattle to graze. While the cattle grazed, boys (working spaces for girls and the songs/tales they learned seem obviously different), taught one another songs, tales, and perhaps many other things. These village commons, usually the clan commons among Kodava and its role in the collective economy of the clan/community have almost vanished in Kodagu given newer land-related individualist economies. What interested me was the manner in which my father, a schoolteacher, connected the local economy and its cultural spaces, and the subsequent changes in economies and in our lives without much nostalgia. Now, with a revivalist zeal many Kodavas, especially the mobile ones outside Kodagu, have turned to learning 'cultural practices' from written books, which is the paradox of economies and cultures.

A pervasive idea around language communities that are oral revolves around the idea of script. The idea that every language needs to have a script of its own seems peculiar to the Indian scenario, circumscribing and limiting orality. Whenever a person of linguistic minority mentions the language s/he speaks, the first question that they encounter is 'does your language have a script? Does your language have a written literature?'. It is not enough for these languages to have begun using a neighbouring script in recent times towards a written lore but there is an insistence on a separate script. Script has almost become a defining criterion for a separate language. In popular and academic perceptions, a language that has not required a script does not qualify to be a language in its own right. The non-necessity of a script in the majority of the world's languages which have continued their knowledge systems in ways other than using the written word is not contextualized nor understood. This predominance of scripturality/obsession with unique script,[20] contradicts the use of Devnagari script (with some variation) for almost all Indo-Aryan languages in India, and the use of Roman script for most European languages.

Shamsur Faruqi's meticulous study on early Urdu literary culture is significant in observing how:

> Since Nagari script was available only to Brahmans, Kayasthas in the 15th century developed a Nagari-based script Kaithi that survived into the 19th century. British promotion of Nagari killed Kaithi. [ ... ] Because of the non-availability of a popular and acceptable script, most of the literature produced in the developing North Indian languages must have been oral. Much of the early use was by Muslims, by Sufis, like Khusrau. (Faruqi 2001, 30)

So indeed, it is because Sanskrit and its script were not accessible, that Hindi and/or Urdu developed. Hindi from this position can be seen as a resistance to Sanskrit. But with the arrival of nationalism that posits worth in unifying/homogenizing religion and language without addressing the inequalities of caste/communities, standardized Hindi has/ is now being used to produce the very same inequalities that Sanskrit

---

[20] Thanks to Mohamed Shafeeq for sharpening this argument.

was part of. This circular manner in which inequalities amongst people are reproduced via language can be effectively addressed via English, a language without a caste memory but with contradictory colonial memories and via empowering of the home language(s) of individuals/smaller communities is what this book will argue in Chapter 3.

All major languages that are also dominant have used the script to propagate the knowledge that they have held important. Along with religion, writing has always been controlled by state power to keep records of administration and revenue/tax. The manner in which this has continued to be powerful in the print economy of today has only pushed languages of minorities into a complicated relationship with languages of nation states and of imperialism made evident in the manner that the Indian state is reorganized on linguistic lines as Devy mentions, where:

> the languages that had scripts were counted. The ones that had not acquired scripts, and therefore did not have printed literature, did not get their own states. Schools and colleges were established only for the official languages. The ones without scripts, even if they had a great stock of wisdom carried forward orally, were not fortunate enough to get educational institutions for them. (Devy 2019, 37)

Sheldon Pollock's *The Language of Gods in the World of Men* begins with a very clear distinction between the oral and the written. It is by now established that literacy and the growth of the culture of writing in South Asia began around 2000 years ago. This change quickly saw the elevation of script and writing from a previous political culture that held orality in high reverence. Pollock makes the distinction between the oral and written by clearly privileging the written. Writing, in his words:

> claims an authority the oral cannot ... The authorization to write, above all to write literature, is no natural entitlement, like the ability to speak, but is typically related to social and political and even epistemological privileges. For another, writing enables textual features far in excess of the oral; for literature it renders the discourse itself a subject for discourse for the first time, language itself an object of aestheticized awareness, the text itself an artefact to be decoded and a pretext for deciphering. In addition, writing makes possible the

production of a history of a sort the oral is incapable of producing. (Pollock 2006, 4)

The elevation of the written through history and literary cultures, Pollock argues, is through the complex network of power and culture. But then, how this power has denigrated orality, not just within the written cultures themselves but especially of communities that lay outside the privileges of the written. This points not to how orality is 'incapable of producing history of a sort that writing can' but to how the many kinds of history that orality constantly produces becomes unwieldy since for practices of history and power, the absolute nature of a written text or inscription lends itself as an easy text. The feelings of the superiority engendered by the written language derive mainly from the 'comparative permanence of writing and because writing for so many centuries [was] a secret craft of priests and learned men' (Le Page 2020, 437). It is also crucial to remember that non-pictographic written language derives from the spoken word. There can never be a written language that preceded the spoken language in human history. Moreover, for contemporary practices based on very positivist and empirical notions of evidence-based history, writing provides easy evidence that evades orality. This very nature of orality that makes history unyielding to power is what according to James Scott is orality's advantages. Using many examples from communities of Southeast Asia, he argues:

> Oral traditions, then, appear to provide, under certain circumstances, something of the word-for-word constancy of a fixed, written text, together with the potential flexibility of strategic adjustment and change. They can, as it were, have it both ways; they can claim to be precise urtext while in fact being substantially novel—and there is no easy way of evaluating this claim. The reasons for strategic and opportunistic adaptation of oral traditions are manifold. Once it is fully appreciated that any account of custom, genealogy, or history is a situated and interested account, variation over time is the presumed norm. (Scott 2009, 232)

Not just this but oral cultures are 'superbly adapted to travel and change ... as shifting cultivation and physical mobility' (Scott 232). These histories that are represented by oral cultures change themselves according to current conditions and contexts. In contrast, a written history freezes one account and passes the very same to future generations as *the* truth. 'The difference is that selective forgetting and remembering is more unobtrusive and smoother in the case of oral tradition' (Scott 234), and of course this selective nature of history is amenable to anyone who has access to the language and not necessarily just people with power. But in the written version, there is never an acknowledgement of its selective nature precisely because it comes with power and authority. To question the veracity of the written word is to question the authority of power itself.

The turn Scott gives in his understanding of orality is to connect orality to people whose political and social organization is communitarian and not based on centralized state systems. Such groups have been historically outside the state system and are 'typically stigmatized by neighbouring cultures as "peoples without history"' (Scott 237).

Although Scott and the recent popular works of Yuval Harari and Rutger Bregman come close to romantic idealism, one cannot push aside the understanding that communities that have been closely knit, who acknowledge their interdependence with each other and with nature are usually the ones who have oral traditions and also tend to be more democratic, more friendly with everything around them. They operate in an economy that is not founded on hierarchies or on accumulation. And this is a conscious choice these communities seem to have made. In effect, this makes orality a crucial political category. In the context of India and its language-communities that have thus far not required writing, but have taken up writing in recent times for various reasons—it is these communities that have held forth an alternate understanding of history, politics, and culture.In short, an alternate understanding of life itself that can counter the contemporary cynicism and extremities of capitalism, patriarchal casteism, and nationalism can emerge from such indigenous communities. This provides us with an alternate understanding of democracy, justice, and equality as Graeber and Wengrow argue in *The Dawn of Everything*.

It is of course true that this book and others that counter the exigencies of writing have used the precise act of writing to do so. Communities that have been largely oral have been using writing and have always been using performative modes for political and cultural purposes and recent writing can also be seen as a strategic use quite unlike and in opposition to the strategies of privileged writing.

Obviously all languages do exist in their oral form, except in cases like Sanskrit in the contemporary world which is hardly spoken in everyday lives and is largely committed to written forms. All languages are spoken first and any other practice is only in addition to its speech form. By orality then, I mean the practices of a language, of a community, and its knowledge that largely exists in its oral and performative forms but is constantly engaging with other forms including writing. What is important to note and what is important for this book is that the practices of orality in our contemporary world have largely been seen as peripheral. These practices are associated with 'illiterate', 'not-so-modern' peripheral people, including practices of lowered caste people, of indigenous/Adivasi communities, of ethnolinguistic minorities, who have been constantly pushed to the margins of states, of power, be it feudal-monarchical or nation. Or, in James Scott's words, many such communities have consciously avoided writing. The orality of a people suggests immediacy and primacy to all speakers of the language. Here, there are no strict hierarchies between religion and everyday practice, there are no mediators between commoners and their beliefs, it is participatory, accessible, democratic, strategic, sustainable with an organic connection with the ecology. This is largely how James Scott uses the term orality and how Ivan Illich understands the vernacular—thereby making a close connection between the oral and the vernacular. There is no distinct division between the performer and listener in orality, they are intimately connected.[21] This to me relates well to Illich's idea of the vernacular which when alienated from subsistence living, alienated and put to use by power, became a language (oral/vernacular) that was perceived 'useless' to knowledge production in the casteist economy of feudal times, and in the contemporary times, useless to capitalist and nationalist desires. So then languages like Kodava, Yerava, Gondi, Ho, and day-to-day usage of languages in the homes of 'impure' or 'illiterate' people are considered useless by the economies of dominant languages around them, continue to be so in some way or the other, albeit in varying degrees. But interestingly, the arrival of English

---

[21] Unlike the orality of Vedic Sanskrit that continues in ritual Hinduism today characterized by a clearly marked hierarchy of caste and gender.

and the failure of the one nation–one language formula has given a new turn to some of these languages.[22]

Although not within the same realm, I use an argument that in a way combines Pollock and Williams—the manner in which they elaborate on how Sanskrit's supremacy was questioned by the growth of vernaculars, in Pollock's case by written vernaculars and in Williams' case by oral compositions., The third chapter in this book argues that minority communities and ethnolinguistic minorities who have taken to the Roman script to write their languages and have embraced knowledge practices of English and of their own language (Khasi and Kodava for example). By doing so, they have not only overridden the dominant vernacular of the region and by doing so, have also challenged the caste-based regional, religious, and nationalist elitism of language and the power of politico-cultural practices. I argue that this challenging of the dominant language and the nationalist languageis many steps ahead of the modernity espoused by writing, by scriptural practices of the elite in the dominant languages, be it Hindi, Kannada, Bangla, or others.

As Pollock and Williams point out, prior to the first century CE Sanskrit circles privileged orality, but the cultural and political power of Sanskrit from the first millennium CE onwards was largely connected to writing. This contradiction is complicated by the fact that Sanskrit's ritualist orality continues within Brahminic circles while simultaneously controlling writing. Williams uses this history of the privilege of writing to explore how Nirgun saints[23] of medieval North India posited their oral compositions to challenge the epistemic, cultural, intellectual, and political privilege of written Sanskrit. The Nirgun saints used the vernaculars in their oral compositions and 'did so by emphasizing the materiality and banality of writing and by characterising inscription as just another form of worldly labour' (Williams 2018, 81).

Williams also points out how poets like Kabir and Ravidas, whom he terms as Nirgun bhakts 'vulgarize writing, robbing of its mystique, returning it to the realm of mundane, and characterizing it as simply another kind of labour, like weaving or leather' (91). These saints

---

[22] Hany Babu (2017).
[23] A form of Bhakti movement that emphasized on the formlessness of God. The most known among the Nirgun saints is Kabir.

consciously foregrounded the experience of intimacy with spoken words that seemed closer to God than the written scripture that was far removed from one's intimacy with God. Most of these saints belonged to the backwarded/lowered castes and were 'illiterate', operating within a literary culture, and consciously worked against the privilege accorded to writing, especially within the then prevalent Persian, Arabic, and Sanskritic literary–culture complex. Williams' argument aligns with Sudipta Kaviraj (2009) in positing a democratic frame to Bhakti poetry and the Bhakti movement in general. An interesting counter is provided by Tharakeshwar who writes:

> the activities of Bhakti tradition and that of colonial missionaries with colonial print capitalism (both colonial and native/nationalist activities) enabled certain languages to be standardized with the coming of print technology and developed the potential to be carriers of linguistic nationalism. (Tharakeshwar 2019, 121)

What is relevant here is the collaboration of the native elite with that of nationalist and colonial elites who appropriated Bhakti in the nineteenth and twentieth centuries. This appropriation of Bhakti and of other 'glorious' traditions of India worked towards standardizing and nationalizing particular languages. What we can also take home is the fact that print colonialism and print nationalism further strengthened the uneven relationships between speech communities.

Novetzke, when discussing the nature of Marathi vernacularization in the thirteenth century, points to how vernacularization of religion (and language) was founded on the basis of the right of everyone to *hear* in one's mother tongue. Terming this as 'sonic equality', Novetzke notes how 'at the confluence of literary vernacularization and the application of a religious ethics of salvation, a discursive sphere opens up in which questions of social equality, particularly around caste and gender, rise to the surface of public debate' (Novetzke 2018, 150). Interestingly for us, this vernacularization engages with orality, in the form of hearing salvational literature in the language of everyday life thus removing it one step away from the stronghold of writing. This one step away from writing and another step ahead of written Sanskrit in the thirteenth century to me can definitely be understood from the framework of modernity that

Pandian proposes. Pandian brings in the voices of the oppressed castes speaking in the twentieth century, his theorizing of modernity, but here in the thirteenth-century Marathi-speaking realm, it is the Brahmin male who is the agent of vernacularization, speaking for lowered castes and/ or women.

If one pays attention to the idea and emergence of 'script', we notice that

'scripture' (from Latin *scriber*, to write) has been closely, even exclusively associated with written documents or holy writ, I wish to include in the concept sacred words, not only in their written or visible form but also in their spoken or sound form. [ ... ] The limitation of 'scripture' to written forms only is sometimes arbitrary, even misleading. Unfortunately, in our literate culture, there is simply no better term to establish a body of sacred work. (Brown 1986, 69)

In Latin and in English the connection between script and scripture is very clear but not so in the other languages with which I am familiar. *Elth* in Kodava, *baraha* in Kannada, *raayu* in Telugu are quite distant from any religious overtones. When I looked up the Sanskrit word for 'write', among many meanings that showed up, *likh* (from *rich*, meaning 'scratch, inscribe') was the most accepted meaning. But what caught my attention were the words *varna* and *granth* as associated with 'write'.[24] The term *granth* in the contemporary context does suggest the religious book. *Varna* we are aware is also the Sanskrit term for 'written alphabet' and significantly also the term for the caste system based on four *varnas*. *Varna* also means colour. This to my mind makes the connection between the caste system and writing quite clear. Put in context, it is only the twice-born males, from the cream of the *varnas* who could access writing and also held ritually and socially superior religious authority. Historical changes and print capitalism with colonialist and nationalist aspirations have only further reinforced the validity of script, furthered by print, and retained its 'pure' connection with twice-born castes. While orality connects itself to the listener within particular spaces, writing has created a

---

[24] http://dictionary.tamilcube.com/sanskrit-dictionary.aspxhttps://sanskritdictionary.com/?iencoding=iast&q=write&lang=sans&action=Search. I also thank Chaitanya Medi and Amba Kulkarni for helping me with this.

kind of distance, 'between the knower and the known and between another reader' (Brown 83), a process in which only some privileged literates could act as mediators, especially in the case of religion the world over. So, with writing, 'word and image has been transcended for at least one brief moment, as the word has become the image of God' (Brown 86), thus retaining the purity of the mediating pure men who controlled knowledge within the economy of religion. Interestingly, there have been arguments from folklorists as to how the written word contaminates the oral. Any oral practice that engages with the written and learns from it in whatever form is seen as contaminating (Niklander 2018, 7). As we will see in Chapter 2 of this book, writing for Nadikerianda Chinnappa, documenting the oral traditions of Kodava would only make the practices pure by standardizing various 'wrongly' practiced customs. Perhaps the difference of positions come into being depending on the person who documents. Who exactly is the documenter, who is the researcher? Do 'outsiders' see a pure culture that can be contaminated? Or do insiders see an already contaminated field? Do insiders, people belonging to oral communities see a dynamic culture that needs to change according to changing contexts? Do they see the need to 'preserve' orality from external factors that contaminate? This question of purity therefore takes many conflicting turns that only suggest how writing is perceived as essential and how one need to justify the acts of writing as pure. As Le Page succinctly puts it: 'the only way to keep yourself pure is by not coming into contact with anybody else; and the only way to keep your language pure is to isolate yourself and never speak to anybody else' (Le Page 2020, 428).

The guarded purity of oral and written Sanskrit in precolonial times is evident and we have seen how colonialism reinforced the cultural capital and purity entrenched in Sanskrit, the language and written 'knowledge' reinforcing its connection to Brahmins with their active collaboration. The manner in which the body of 'Indian literature' was recovered and constituted via Sanskrit, the manner in which Sanskrit texts were translated, the manner in which it was studied making connections with the pure Aryan races, and instituted in institutions across the world, furthered the continuities of Sanskrit in newer ways. Purity associated with caste, associated with the written word, and associated with uniformity which is so very desired by any form of governance is further standardized exclusively in written forms via translation during colonial times.

Although purity of written language was maintained and also its written uniformity—this was limited to the court's language and the religious language (be it Sanskrit, Arabic, or Persian) and not the vernaculars, the spoken languages of the people. Although many vernaculars went through vernacularization much before colonialism, the debate around the vernaculars and the manner in which it had to be part of the governance system is what was new during colonialism. This varies from and complicates the argument James Scott makes that most indigenous people whom he refers to as post-literate have, to a large extent, avoided dominant forms of governance that used written histories. In contrast, the modes of governance in post-literate indigenous societies are oral, in languages that are not accessible to the dominant state-based languages. Needless to say these oral modes and the languages in which they operate, the communities to which they belong are minorities in terms of numbers and in terms of its sociopolitical power in relation to dominant society. This to dominant forms of governance seems chaotic, seems impure since it is accessed by everyone and not restricted to an elite caste/class; not controlled by anyone. Since it is also only the elite who control the power of writing and control power via writing, it is evident that even within these languages of control, a majority of the very same speech communities that speak non-standardized forms of language (termed impure), become peripheral. These peripheral people, restricted to oral, performative, and productive modes of economy are usually people belonging to the lowered castes is a foregone conclusion. This is how governance operated in majoritarian languages be it within East Asian, or South Asian societies. This is also a power that the colonizer's languages sought to take control of resulting in different effects on different caste communities. Anindita Ghosh, B. Kar, D. R. Nagaraj, Janaki Nair, M. S. S. Pandian, D. L Sheth, and S. Kaviraj have shown us how it is not just the colonizer but the Indian elite, too, who reinforced and followed this argument for a 'pure' written language that would not only consolidate identities within the structures of caste in mainstream Indian societies but would provide them with a vernacularized language equipped with rich written history, written literature, presumably older than that of the colonizer. A combination of this rich written history with an emerging contemporary prose based on the languages of regional and caste elites waiting to be standardized attempted to counter the colonizer's myth of civilizational superiority and refashioned a civilizational myth as against the ethnolinguistic and caste minorities.

It was not the long literary and associated written intellectual history in Sanskrit or in a few vernacularized languages of India that a majority of people of the subcontinent associated themselves with. For many ethnolinguistic minorities and for the lowered castes, written textuality was introduced by the British. Therefore, the power of writing took a different form at a point when the religious power of Sanskrit, or Arabic, or Persian plus courtly power got taken over by English. English and writing (even in the dominant vernacular) made accessible to all through formal education exposed minority communities to a different intellectuality whose ideals at least suggested equality and mobility outside the caste society. It also opened the world of the language cultures of these people to a world outside, blinkered by the Sanskritic rules of erstwhile powers.

Given this complex history of orality and its connection to writing in India, today ironically, the oral is almost exclusively identified with Adivasi/tribal/ethnolinguistic communities. 'While most tribal narratives are classified as folklore, and not literature' (Choksi 2018, 92), implying folklore as connected to oral, tribal, and folklore studies, literature has been associated with the literate and literary studies. Choksi further points out how even Sahitya Akademi, affirms the close, indistinguishable relation between tribal and oral. In an ironic turn of histories suggesting a Herderian idea, this connection between oral and tribal has 'displaced Adivasi practices onto the realm of "pure culture"—rendering these practices resistant to interpretative use by historians and in turn preventing the adequate political mobilization of such practices' (Choksi 2018, 92). Choksi's objective then in his article is to show how the Adivasis have long engaged with the script, in fact engaged with multiple scriptural traditions, thereby 'contesting long-held stereotypes that grounds Adivasi cultural identity primarily in oral traditions' (92). Basing his argument on the Roman, Bengali, Devnagari, and Ol-Chiki scripts that Santals engage with and its connection to the identity of Santals, Choksi argues that the newly created scripts 'mediate histories and spiritual relations while at the same time incorporating elements of both Sanskritic and European literary practices' (2018, 93). Although Choksi tries to break the stereotype of the tribal connection with oral, he himself notes that these scriptural traditions are new and a product of the history of colonization and

missionary activity in the eastern parts of India. The question for us is
how and why was script not central to Santal identity until around two
hundred years ago? What makes script so easily available with colonization and Christianity which earlier associations of tribal culture (or that
of Sanskritic cultures around) could not?

> As Brahmin derived scripts are associated with dominant institutions
> in addition to maintaining a sound to script ideology that is associated
> with upper-caste language and practice, many Santals, especially those
> active in language politics view scripts as the purview of upper-caste
> Hindus. (Choksi 97)

Two things can be gleaned from Choksi's argument. That indeed Santals
have engaged with scripts in recent years, particularly after colonization and the advent of Christianity; that the scriptural traditions of the
caste communities around them prior to this recent history, is viewed as
a mode of power and hierarchy. We need to constantly remind ourselves
that most people not just in India but all over the world have taken to
writing only recently. This perhaps explains the move of many Santals
who inhabit many linguistically divided states towards the Roman script
and the more recent new script, Ol-Chiki, a script of their own. Like
Skaria before him shows, and as Choksi himself argues, in addition to
James Scott's arguments, tribals have always used various strategies when
it came to writing. Never did they view their own practices of orality as
unchanging or as incapable of carrying the burden of history. Within the
contemporary necessities of changing economy, ecology, and politics,
how the many tribes of India have adopted or are adopting practices of
writing or asserting their identities through other performative practices
in continuation with their existing oral traditions is a matter for us to take
up. Linda Hess in her discussion on Kabir's songs says:

> Beyond the oral and the written, we have to think about multidirec-
> tional transmission via bodies, objects, devices; texts walking, flying,
> embracing and repelling each other, getting written and printed, mag-
> netized, and digitized, and turning again into live performances. The
> question arises: Amidst all this media cacophony, does the term 'oral
> tradition' have any meaning? (Hess 2017, 46)

Recognizing the problems with the question she raises, her answer to the question is yes. Orality for Hess 'entails live, body-to-body transmission, [ … ] They entail a certain fluidity of text, a certain unpredictability of content and interaction. Printed texts (or inscribed ones) are fixed, can be individually owned and returned to, and are normally consumed privately' (Hess 46). This and the democratic nature of orality (and to some extent digital media) that everyone can access and own has the nature of public embedded into it. For Hess, unlike the written word which has the authority of the author and of power, 'Orality implies sociality, which can be dispensed within consumption of print and other fixed portable media' (46). To this, I would only wish to add the kinds of power orality, vernacular, and writing carry between them; the kinds of knowledges they produce and the manner in which they are valued in today's world.

That today, language needs to be written is a given. Although many languages have survived thousands of years without the necessity of using the script, the economy and the contexts in which they survived were entirely different. There were languages of gods, languages of religion, languages of the court, languages of political and cultural expansion including colonialism and nationalism, that exclusively held the power of writing. 'Lesser' languages were used in different modes, performative, day-to-day, skill-based, production-based, material, and survived in their own locales until the arrival of new economies connected to colonialism, capitalism, and nation states that required strengthened surveillance and record-keeping of their subjects and of the profits accrued by capitalist industry. Linguistic minorities and other minorities who were until recently based in specific locales, restricted to caste community-based occupations, with no access to privileged knowledge of the script, have begun to be mobile/migrants, sometimes in very difficult and disempowering conditions. This requires new understandings of the practices of language. One way of using language when alienated from the community is to use it in writing (or typing through social media). Although one can notice how the visual media operates in myriad ways in the current world of the Internet thereby giving a platform for practices other than script, giving an altogether new twist to the oral and performative, the sacrosanct nature of script has continued to maintain its privilege. Nishaant Choksi's arguments towards seeing Santali as a language and people whose identity is circumscribed by scripturality of many kinds only reinforces the centrality of script within structures of power, the centrality of caste in the case of India. What I think is useful is that we pursue a method that brings together many ways of expression and reveals the network of strategies and power that operate among speech communities.

## Orality as a Method

There has been much work on orality, paradoxically in the written form. This work tries to revisit the manner in which languages are studied and the implications they have in understanding history and identity. Since writing and written history are inseparably connected, I wish to work with orality, especially as practised by linguistic minorities, so as to understand how orality and translation can indeed provide us with alternative perspectives and methods to dominant written histories and historiographies.

Among many scholars whose work on orality has been influential, I draw from Wendy Singer who points out that 'oral narratives are *not* the same as simple, unself-reflective memory [ ... ]. They are deliberately structured by their tellers for immediate purposes and audiences' (Singer 1997, 7). The arguments in this work are also hugely inspired by James Scott who not only makes connections between orality and history but also shows how practitioners of orality are also practitioners of a more egalitarian economy and polity.

> If swiddening and egalitarian, mobile settlement represent elusive 'jellyfish' economic and social forms, orality may be seen as a similarly fugitive jellyfish variant of culture. On this reading, orality may in many cases be a 'positionality' vis- à-vis state formation and state power. (Scott 2009, 220–221)

Throughout this work, I am guided by how Scott views orality as much more democratic than written cultures. Scott provides us with two reasons.

> First, the ability to read and write is typically less broadly distributed than the ability to tell stories. Second, there is rarely any simple way to

'adjudicate' among variant tellings of oral history; certainly there is no fixed, written text to which the variants can be compared for veracity. [ … ] The spoken word, like language itself, is a collectivist activity inasmuch as its conventions have to be shared by whole groups of societies of varying size. In fact, in the case of oral histories and narratives, the concept of 'the original' simply does not make any sense. (Scott 2009, 230)

Scott further argues how people who have thus far largely used oral forms are 'typically stigmatized by neighboring cultures as "peoples without history", as lacking the fundamental characteristic of civilization, namely historicity', Scott rejects this 'lack' on two counts. First being that this notion stigmatizes orality by assuming that only written history counts in order to build a narrative of identity and of a past. Second and, 'more important, how much history a people have, far from indicating their low stage of evolution, is always an active choice, one that positions them vis-à-vis their powerful text-based neighbors' (Scott 237). In effect, this also opens up the field of written history as being an active choice, invested with choice, the difference being in the matter of power that written cultures have exercised over oral cultures, at least in the last two millennia.

Arguing for a method that recognizes a constant interaction between the oral and written in languages of India, G. N. Devy shows how this 'pre-existent written, or a simultaneity of the oral and the written', challenges the historiography of writing (Devy 2019, 327). Despite the challenge to dominant historiographies of writing, Devy to some extent romanticizes a past whose practices seem much more fluid, a past that was changed by colonization.

Anindita Ghosh, charting out how a particular 'genteel' language was pitted against the 'colloquial' in the making of vernacular literatures of India, frames her work on the basis of how the early nineteenth-century attempts to purify Bengali were laden with the ideologies of 'enlightened' male consciousness that 'shifted the burden of "vulgarity" to less privileged social groups' (Ghosh 2006, 4), and argues, 'specific boundaries of genteel distinction had not been so rigid in the pre-print period' (4), and how writing was essential for prescriptive notions of class and gentility.

What means are available to us to understand orality that points to alternate practices, alternate to that of the power relations embedded within written traditions? What are the implications of the contradictions that at once see orality as undesirable and as expressing the 'purest' sentiments of folk? I do not aim to do the impossible—study the thousands of oral cultures that exist around us. I only aim to understand how the orality around us has been constructed and how we can understand them in newer ways. It is the discourse around orality that interests me and its connection to the scripted/printed word that has implications for our being. In doing this, I am indebted to Talal Asad's proposition:

> The purpose of this criticism, therefore, is to further a collective endeavor. Criticizing 'savages who are after all some distance away' [*orality in our case*] in an ethnographic monograph they cannot read, does not seem to me to have the same kind of purpose. In order for criticism to be responsible, it must always be addressed to someone who can contest it. (Asad1986, 156. Words in square brackets and italics are mine)

Following this, my critique is around the discourse of orality and the kind of ab/uses it has been put to. The hope is that we engage with practices that acknowledge the power enmeshed in acts of writing (including this very work), and work towards listening/watching to a variety of utterances. What I think might work is to see writing as fluid, the 'truth' in writing as fluid, as much as these hold true for orality as well. We also need to 'see' writing as an act of translation (which is also fluid), as a representation from the moment it is conceived and put down in words to the moments it is infinitely interpreted. It is therefore not just in deconstructing the sacredness of writing, already deconstructed in lived practices, but also in looking at the systems of knowledge based on orality in its negotiation with other knowledge practices. It is in understanding systems of knowledge that sustain a decentralized political–communitarian commons; systems that need not imagine the homogeneity of the nation state; that we can perhaps build many new commons by moving away from caste-based, capitalist economies, that we can envision a method and life that is more equal.

## What Do I Mean by Languages of the Minority or Ethnolinguistic Minorities?

Although the focus of this work is largely Adivasi communities and ethnolinguistic minorities, I also wish to bring into the picture the largely oral nature of knowledge of the lowered-caste people and/or women for whom until recently any privileged knowledge, especially in Sanskrit, especially in writing, was not made accessible. The irony today is that literature in the dominant languages/vernacularized languages of India is largely written by the lowered caste while English has become the higher caste's expressive language. The irony continues in the aspiration for English among the lowered castes. The vernacularized linguistic identity that potentially overcomes other divisive identities in a particular region has been to some extent successful in both questioning caste while simultaneously also being used to propagate casteist structures. The ethnolinguistic minority and Adivasi communities that have taken up English and their own tongues instead of the dominant vernacular have to some extent avoided the trap of caste inherent in the dominant languages of India.

The states and the caste communities that have held political and cultural power have hardly acknowledged the knowledge practices outside the realm of power, outside the realm of writing, and in fact have actively dismissed them. The knowledge practices of these peripheral communities were until recently never committed to writing and this does not just include the practices of Adivasis and ethnolinguistic minorities but also that of productive castes, castes lowered in the hierarchy.

I see a difference between a linguistic minority and languages of minority. One good example is Urdu—which does not necessarily belong to a linguistic minority (the number of people who speak Urdu is quite large) but it is a language belonging to a minoritized group of people. Sometimes the number of people who speak the language matters, sometimes it is the sociopolitical power that decides who is a minority. This book does not necessarily deal with languages of religious minorities. And 'minorities' in the book do not necessarily mean religious minorities. It also includes people minoritized by caste and community. Language and politics of religious minorities might need another book. There can be different kinds of linguistic minorities and can include both the context and geography specific. Sometimes it so happens that the speakers of one language are a minority at one level but at another, they are a majority. For example, let's say there is a considerable Kannada-speaking population in Tamil Nadu and they are considered linguistics minorities; but in Karnataka, Kannada speakers are definitely not linguistic minorities. There are contexts where speakers of some languages remain minority at all levels. If you consider a Balti speaker from Kashmir as a linguistic minority or that they belong to the languages of minority (since Baltis are also ethnolinguistic minority/Adivasi/indigenous community in addition to their language being a language of minority since most of them are practitioners of Islam),—they are a minority at every level, also a minority in relation to Kashmiri and Urdu. There are religious minorities, Urdu speakers, there are Telugu speakers in Karnataka who are linguistic minorities, and ethnic minorities like Parsis or Anglo Indians who might speak Guajarati or English but are still minorities of a special kind. Linguistic minorities can belong to different kinds of classification. Therefore in my usage, languages of minority can mean any of the above or an overlapping of all the above mentioned categories; the non-standardized speech forms of lowered castes to the languages that have numerically less number of people to the languages of people who are minorities of different kinds. I have tried my best to illustrate contextual differences as and when these usages demand in this book.

I also wish to note that the terms 'tribes'/'Adivasis'/'ethnolinguistic minorities'/'indigenous', are used interchangeably in this book. These are categories that are wrought and no commonly acceptable understanding of these terms are current.

# References

Abbi, Anvita (ed). 1997. *Languages of Tribal and Indigenous Peoples of India: The Ethnic Space*. Delhi: Motilal Banarasidas Publishers Private Limited.

Agnihotri, Rama Kant. 2022. 'Negotiating Multilinguality'. In *Being and Becoming Multilingual: Some Narratives*, eds Rajesh Sachdeva and Rama Kant Agnihotri, pp. 286–308. Hyderabad: Orient Blackswan.

Ambedkar, B. R. 1955. *Thoughts on Linguistic States of India*. http://ambedkar.org/ambcd/05A.%20Thoughts%20on%20Linguistic%20States%20Part%20I.htm

Asad, Talal.1986. 'The Concept of Cultural Translation in British Social Anthropology'. In *Writing Culture: The Poetics and Politics of Ethnography*, eds James Clifford and

George E. Marcus, pp. 141–164. Berkeley and Los Angeles, CA: University of California Press.

Babu, Hany. 2017. 'Breaking the Chaturvarna System of Languages The Need to Overhaul the Language Policy'. *Economic and Political Weekly* 52 (23): 112–119.

Banerjee, Prathama. (2016). 'Writing the Adivasi: Some Historiographical Notes'. *Indian Economic and Social History Review* 53 (1): 131–153.

Barkhade, Dipak Mangalbhai. 2022. 'Constituting "Standard Public" and "Alternative Public": A Study of the Discourse around Language and Identity in Selected Bundeli Texts'. Unpublished PhD Thesis. Hyderabad: University of Hyderabad.

Baumann, Richard and Charles Briggs. 2003. *Voices of Modernity: Language Ideologies and the Politics of Inequality*. Cambridge: Cambridge University Press.

Bhattacharya, S. S. 2002. 'Languages in India—Their Status and Function'. In *Linguistic Landscaping in India with Particular Reference to the New States*, eds N. H. Itagi and Shailendra Kumar Singh, pp. 54–97. Mysore: Central Institute of Indian Languages.

Boldrini, Lucia. 2010. 'Comparative Literature and Translation, Historical Breaks and Continuing Debates: Can the Past Teach us Something about the Future?'. *Diacrítica. Dossier Literatura Comparada* 24 (3): 181–199.

Bourdieu, Pierre. 1991. *Language and Symbolic Power*. Harvard, MA: Harvard University Press.

Brass, Paul. 2009. 'Elite Interests, Popular Passions, and Social Power in the Language Politics of India'. In *Language and Politics in India*, ed. Asha Sarangi, pp. 183–220. New Delhi: Oxford University Press.

Bregman, Rutger. 2021. *Humankind: A Hopeful History*, trans. Elizabeth Manton and Erica Moore. London: Bloomsbury.

Bright, William (ed.). 1966. *Sociolinguistics: Proceedings of the UCLA Sociolinguistics Conference, 1964*. The Hague: Mouton.

Brown, Mackenzie. 1986. 'Purana as Scripture: From Sound to Image of the Holy Word in the Hindu Tradition'. *History of Religions* 26 (1): 68–86.

Butalia, Urvashi. 2000. *The Other Side of Silence: Voices From the Partition of India*. London: Hurst and Company.

Casanova, Pascale. 2004. *The World Republic of Letters*, trans. M. B. Debevoise. Harvard, MA: Harvard University Press.

Choksi, Nishaant. 2018. 'Script as Constellation Among Munda Speakers: The Case of Santhali'. *South Asian History and Culture* 9 (1): 92–115.

Cohn, S. Bernard. 1985. 'The Command of Language and the Language of Command'. In *Subaltern Studies IV: Writings on South Asian History and Society*, ed. Ranajit Guha, pp. 276–329. New Delhi: Oxford University Press.

Cronin, Michael. 2009. 'The Cracked Looking Glass of Servants: Translation and Minority Languages in a Global Age'. In *Translation Studies: Critical Concepts in Linguistics*, Vol. 4, ed. Mona Baker, pp. 3–21. New York: Routledge.

Dev, Amiya. 2019. 'Multilingualism and India's Literary Culture'. In *Multilingualism and the Literary Cultures of India*, ed. M. T. Ansari, pp. 3–13. New Delhi: Sahitya Akademi.

Devy, G. N. 2019. 'Language Diversity in India'. In *Multilingualism and the Literary Cultures of India*, ed. M. T. Ansari, pp. 29–48. New Delhi: Sahitya Akademi.

Emeneau, M. B. 1994a. 'The Languages of the Nilgiris'. In *Dravidian Studies: Selected Papers*Ed. Bh. Krishnamurthy, pp. 387–398. Delhi: Motilal Banarsidas Publishers.

Faruqi, Shamsur Rahman. 2001. *Early Urdu Literary Culture*. New Delhi: Oxford University Press.

Foucault, Michel. 1979. 'What Is an Author?'. In *Textual Strategies*, ed. Josue V. Harari, pp. 141–160. New York: Cornell University Press.

Ghosh, Anindita. 2006. *Power in Print: Popular Publishing and Politics of Language and Culture in a Colonial Society*. New Delhi: Oxford University Press.

Guha, Ranjit. 1996. 'The Small Voice of History'. In *Subaltern Studies IX: Writings on South Asian History and Society*, eds Shahid Amin and Dipesh Chakrabarty, pp. 1–12. Delhi: Oxford University Press.

Harari, Yuval. 2015. *Sapiens: A Brief History of Humankind*. London: Vintage.

Hess, Linda. 2017. 'When a Text is a Song'. In *Multilingual Nation: Translation and Language Dynamics in India*e, ed. Rita Kothari, pp. 25–49. New Delhi: Oxford University Press.

Illich, Ivan. 1980. 'Vernacular Values'. http://www.davidtinapple.com/illich/1980_ve rnacular_values.html. Accessed 12 September 2018.

Jaaware, Aniket. 2019. *Practicing Caste: On Touching and Not Touching*. Hyderabad: Orient Blackswan.

Jaffe, Alexandra. 2009. 'Locating Power: Corsican Translators and their Critics'. In *Translation Studies: Critical Concepts in Linguistics*, Vol. 4, ed. Mona Baker, pp. 22–46. New York: Routledge.

Jain, Jasbir. 2019. 'My Mother's House has Many Mansions, but the Windows are Too Few'. In *Multilingualism and the Literary Cultures of India*, ed. M. T. Ansari, pp. 14–28. New Delhi: Sahitya Akademi.

Joseph, Tony. 2018. *Early Indians: The Story of our Ancestors and Where We Came From*. New Delhi: Juggernaut.

Kar, Bodhisattva. 2008. '"Tongue Has No Bone": Fixing the Assamese Language, *c.* 1800–*c.* 1930'. *Studies in History* 24 (1): 27–76.

Kaviraj, Sudipta. 2009. 'Writing, Speaking, Being: Language and the Historical Formation of Identities in India'. In *Language and Politics in India*, ed. Asha Sarangi, pp. 312–350. New Delhi: Oxford University Press.

Kaviraj, Sudipta. 2010. *The Imaginary Institution of India: Politics and Ideas*. New York: Columbia University Press.

Khubchandani, M. Lachman. 2002. 'Language Profiles of Jharkhand, Chhattisgarh and Uttaranchal: A Subaltern Perspective of Language Development'. In *Linguistic Landscaping in India with Particular Reference to the New States*, eds N. H. Itagi and Shailendra Kumar Singh, pp. 98–107. Mysore: Central Institute of Indian Languages.

King, R. Christopher. 1994. *One Language Two Scripts: The Hindi Movement in Nineteenth Century North India*. New Delhi: Oxford University Press.

Kothari, Rita. 2017a. 'Introduction'. In *The Multilingual Nation: Translation and Language Dynamics in India*, ed. Rita Kothari, pp. 1–24. New Delhi: Oxford University Press.

Kuttaiah, Pranav. 2018. 'Are Linguistic Nationalisms Killing South Indian Federalism?'. *Economic and Political Weekly* 53 (46). https://www.epw.in/engage/

article/are-linguistic-nationalisms-killing-south-indian-federalism. Accessed 6 August 2020.

Le Page, Robert B. 2020. *Language and Identity. Selected Papers of Robert B. Le Page*, eds Rama Kant Agnihotri, Mahendra Kishore Verma, and Vandana Puri. Hyderabad: Orient Blackswan.

Littau, Karin. 2000. 'Pandora's Tongues'. *Traduction, Terminologie, Redaction* 13 (1): 21–35.

Mallikarjun, B. 1993. *A Descriptive Analysis of Yerava*. Mysore: Central Institute of Indian Languages.

Martin, J. R. 2008. 'Incongruent and Proud: De-vilifying "nominalization"'. *Discourse & Society* 19 (6): 801–810.

Mitchell, Lisa. 2009. *Language, Emotion, and Politics in South India: The Making of a Mother Tongue*. Ranikhet: Permanent Black.

Mohan, Sanal. 2015. *Modernity of Slavery: Struggles against Caste Inequality in Colonial Kerala*. New Delhi: Oxford University Press.

Murmu, Ganesh. 2002. 'Development of Santali Language, Literature and its Recognition (Language/Script Movement)'. In *Linguistic Landscaping in India with Particular Reference to the New States*, eds N. H. Itagi and Shailendra Kumar Singh, pp. 242–255. Mysore: Central Institute of Indian Languages.

Nagaraj, D. J. 2012. *Listening to the Loom. Essays on Literature, Politics and Violence*, ed. Prithvi Datta Chandra Shobhi. New Delhi: Permanent Black.

Nair, Janaki. 2009. 'Language and the Right to the City'. In *Language and Politics in India*, ed. Asha Sarangi, pp. 368–415. Delhi: Oxford University Press.

Nair, Janaki. 2011. *Mysore Modern. Rethinking the Region under Princely Rule*. Hyderabad: Orient Blackswan.

Nagaraj, D. R. 2012. *Listening to the Loom. Essays on Literature, Politics and Violence*, ed. Prithvi Datta Chandra Shobhi. New Delhi: Permanent Black.

Niklander, Kirti Salmi, Pertti Anttonen, and Cecilia Af Forsellas. 2018. *Oral Tradition and Book Culture*. Helsinki: Finnish Literature Society.

Novetzke, Christian Lee. 2018. 'Religion and Public Sphere in Premodern India'. *ASIA* 72 (1): 147–176.

Orsini, Francesca. 2017. 'Na Hindu Na Turk: Shared Languages, Accents, and Located Meanings'. In *The Multilingual Nation: Translation and Language Dynamics in India*, ed. Rita Kothari, pp. 50–69. New Delhi: Oxford University Press.

Orsini, Francesca. 2020. 'Vernacular: Flawed but Necessary?'. *South Asian Review* 41 (2): 204–206.

Pandian M. S. S. 2002. 'One Step Outside Modernity: Caste, Identity Politics and Public Sphere'. *Economic and Political Weekly* 37 (18): 1735–1741.

Parpola, Asko. 1994. *Deciphering the Indus Script*. Cambridge: Cambridge University Press.

Patel, P. G. 1996. 'Linguistic and Cognitive Aspects of the Orality–Literacy Complex in Ancient India'. *Language and Communication* 16 (4): 315–329.

Pegu, Manoranjan. 2020. https://www.theHindu.com/opinion/lead/striking-a-blow-against-assams-inclusive-ethos/article31965577.ece

Pollock, Sheldon. 1998. 'The Cosmopolitan Vernacular'. *The Journal of Asian Studies* 57 (1): 6–37.

Pollock, Sheldon. 2006. *The Language of the Gods in the World of Men*. Delhi: Permanent Black.

Prasad, Madhava. 2014. 'The Political Commons: Language and the Nation State Form'. *Critical Quarterly* 56 (3): 92–105.

Rai, Alok. 2001. *Hindi Nationalism*. Hyderabad: Orient Longman.

Ramanujan, A. K. 1991. 'Three Hundred Rāmāyaṇas: Five Examples and Three Thoughts on Translation'. In *Many Rāmāyaṇas: The Diversity of a Narrative Tradition in South Asia*, ed. Paula Richman, pp. 22–48. Berkeley, CA: University of California Press.

Ramaswamy, Sumathy. 1997. *Passions of the Tongue: Language Devotion in Tamil India, 1891–1970*. Berkeley, CA: University of California Press.

Richman, Paula. 1991. *Many Ramayanas. The Diversity of a Narrative Tradition in South Asia*, ed. Paula Richman. Berkeley, CA: University of California Press.

Satchidanandan, K. 2019. 'Living with Many Tongues'. In *Multilingualism and the Literary Cultures of India*, ed. M. T. Ansari, pp. 63–69. New Delhi: Sahitya Akademi.

Scott, James. 2009. *The Art of Not Being Governed. An Anarchist History of Upland Southeast Asia*. Hyderabad: Orient Blackswan.

Scott, Joan W. 1991. 'The Evidence of Experience'. *Critical Inquiry* 17 (4): 773–797.

Sengupta, Madhumita. 2017. 'Representing Kamrupi: Ideologies of Grammar and the Question of Linguistic Boundaries'. In *The Multilingual Nation: Translation and Language Dynamics in India*, ed. Rita Kothari, pp. 172–195. New Delhi: Oxford University Press.

Shankar, S. 2012. *Flesh and Fish Blood: Postcolonialism, Translation and the Vernacular*. Berkeley and Los Angeles, CA: California University Press.

Shankar, S. 2020. 'The Vernacular: An Introduction'. *South Asian Review* 41 (2): 191–193.

Shashidhar, Karthik. 2018. 'Nagaland Is the Most Diverse State In India, Language-Wise'. Livemint, 11 July, https://www.livemint.com/Politics/N5QQIaSOB5GVUMP 0IM3f6K/Nagaland-is-the-most-diverse-state-in-India-language-wise.html.

Sheth, D. L. 2009. 'The Great Language Debate: Politics of Metropolitan versus Vernacular India'. In *Language and Politics in India*, ed. Asha Sarangi, pp. 267–298. New Delhi: Oxford University Press.

Singer, Wendy. 1997. *Creating Histories: Oral Narratives and the Politics of History-Making*. New Delhi: Oxford University Press.

Skaria, Ajay. 1996. 'Writing, Orality and Power in the Dangs, Western India, 1800s–1920s'. In *Subaltern Studies IX: Writings on South Asian History and Society*, eds Shahid Amin and Dipesh Chakrabarty, pp. 13–58. Delhi: Oxford University Press.

Somayyaji, Pattabhirama. 2002. 'Chartering Carceral Society: Kodagu-Linguistically Speaking'. In *Linguistic Landscaping in India with Particular Reference to the New States*, eds N. H. Itagi and Shailendra Kumar Singh, pp. 139–153. Mysore: Central Institute of Indian Languages.

Stovall, Tyler. 2018. https://www.historians.org/publications-and-directories/persp ectives-on-history/september-2018/hayden-v-white-(1928%E2%80%932018)

Tharakeshwar, V. B. 2019. 'Historical Multilingual Landscape of India: Through the Prism of Literary Translations'. In *Multilingualism and the Literary Cultures of India*, ed. M. T. Ansari, pp. 114–134. New Delhi: Sahitya Akademi.

Trivedi, Harish. 2019. 'Multilingualism in India: Some Questions and Caveats'. In *Multilingualism and the Literary Cultures of India*, ed. M. T. Ansari, pp. 49–62. New Delhi: Sahitya Akademi.

White, Hayden. 1992. 'Historiography as Narration'. In *Telling Facts: History and Narration in Psychoanalysis*, eds Joseph H. Smith and Humphrey Morris, pp. 284–300. Baltimore: Johns Hopkins University Press.

Williams, Tyler. 2018. 'If the Whole World Eere Paper: A History of Writing in the North India Vernacular'. *History and Theory*. Theme Issue 56: 81–101.

Xaxa, Virginius. 1999. 'Transformation of Tribes in India'. *Economic and Political Weekly* 34 (24): 1519–1524.

# 1

# Colonial and Nationalist Construction of Language

## The Minority Question

I grew up in Somawarapete, north Kodagu (or Coorg as it is popularly known) where Kannada speakers outnumbered Kodava and other linguistic groups. One of the questions Kodava-speaking students like me always had to face was 'why is your Kannada bad?'. (By bad, it was understood it didn't adhere to the spoken Kannada prevalent in and around Somawarapete.) This question was kind of reversed when I went to Mangalore and Mysore for higher studies, where we, Kodava speakers were asked: 'why is your English better than your Kannada?' and in addition, 'does your language have a script?'. These questions are asked even today by academics and commoners alike without reflecting on how people who speak a particular language at home and are educated in another language at school might find a learning gap that is very difficult to bridge. And also, as discussed in the introduction, it is not necessary to have a script in order for it to be considered or classified as a language. I also want to add that spoken languages at home, even if they are the same as the language of the school, are sometimes quite alien to children (especially for those who are less endowed) because the school language, the text books, and the discourse is so standardized (often Sanskritized in the Indian context) that a child finds it alienating. Not just alienating, these gaps further lead to ideas of who are meritorious and who are deserving students is another story to tell. But then, why do Kodavas perform better in English than in Kannada, even as neither of the two was/is the language spoken in our homes. A handful of Kodava speakers might have been up the social ladder, but for a majority of us, we had no cultural capital connected to English whatsoever. This question of how most

*Languages of Minority*. Sowmya Dechamma CC, Oxford University Press. © Oxford University Press 2024.
DOI: 10.1093/oso/9780198908456.003.0002

Kodava speakers engaged with English much more *aspirationally* than with Kannada has stuck with me to this day. What are the possible histories that have propelled this engagement with English? While Chapter Three analyses this question of engagement with English, this chapter is a precursor to it, looking at the history that laid the ground work that made such an aspiration possible. My effort in this chapter is to see how colonial modes enabled languages that function within domains of smaller communities to be used in roles thus far not used, and made them visible in the public by institutionalizing them through their documentation and study. How did the colonizers construct many such languages like the Kodava? Were all representations orientalist in nature? How did certain representations and forms of knowledge constructed by nineteenth-century Europeans paint ethnolinguistic minorities as different and what implications did this have for the people who spoke these languages is what concerns this chapter. The chapter also looks at how nationalist elites across India talked about their own languages and also of others. In their efforts to build an identity that suited the ideals of a modern nation state, language became a fraught category, both for the colonial and nationalist scholars.

This chapter will look at the various contradictory ways in which Europeans and Indian nationalist elites have written and represented the peoples and the languages these people spoke, were educated in, or with which they were familiar. Basing my analysis on representations from various texts from the mid-to-late nineteenth and early twentieth centuries, I explore how the focus at times is the lack of written literature and written history among the ethnolinguistic minorities and how these communities are seen as unlettered and 'uncivilized'. At other times, the representations speak of the unlettered communities as having a morally higher ground than that of lettered and 'civilized' communities. Some of the writings, especially the colonial officials (and occasionally the nationalist elites) mention the role of Brahmins who had absolute control of the skills of written language and therefore held the reins of knowledge within their community, thereby representing most sections of society in their writings according to what best suited their caste interests. What also emerge as patterns in these works are the unclear distinctions between language and dialects, the lettered and unlettered (scripted and oral), connections between language, race and people, and aspects of purity associated by the nationalist elite with certain languages. More importantly, aspects of democracy and equality associated with languages also emerge as crucial notions. The questions running through this chapter are: how these constructions of language cannot necessarily be understood as orientalist, and how they can also be understood as informed by a caste hierarchy. The relationship of the colonizer and that of ethnolinguistic minorities also defies a linear understanding. As the analysis of the texts show, this engagement with the colonizer can only be understood by complicating the nationalist discourse. The colonizers' differentiating the tribes or ethnolinguistic minorities from the Brahminical order, their construction of Brahmin as the outsider, the construction of the folk literature of these communities as not so tainted by Hindu scriptures, not always equating these languages and their non-literate characteristic as 'primitive', are only a few among the many examples that make us rethink nationalist, anti-colonial narratives. What also makes us rethink nationalist concerns are the views on languages as democratic tools that are posited by nationalist elites while there are other nationalists whose views on language are embedded with notions of hierarchy marked by caste and caste purity. What emerges from the analysis is a very unclear, nonlinear, often contradictory and blurred notions of orientalist/nationalist representations. The representations are at once exotic, demeaning, and condescending, but then they also make languages visible, enabling them with an attempt to democratize the language community realm.

There exists a considerable body of literature in English by grammarians, orientalists, colonial administrators, missionaries, and Indian elites in the nineteenth and twentieth centuries who constructed varied ideas of what 'small' languages are and narrated the history of the speakers of these languages in the texts they produced. Although there is an equally huge body of literature by nationalist elites on the language question, much of these are in the languages to which the particular nationalists belong and therefore not accessible to me, except when they are in English, Kannada, or Kodava. Therefore, I have used secondary sources to understand the nationalist engagement with language during the late nineteenth and early twentieth centuries. By secondary sources I mean research studies that have placed language in their historical and political contexts by using primary sources from particular languages. In the texts written and compiled by colonizers, my focus is largely on the languages of the minority, languages spoken by ethnic minorities and by communities known as Tribes or Adivasis and also the languages spoken by people of oppressed caste groups, often attributed as non-standardized or dialects. I also wish to note that the selections I have made here are by no means representative of the debates around languages. This also makes the case that language and the discourse around it is very fluid, with no ideology that can be said to have taken a stronghold. But then, we do notice a couple of things: very rarely do we find representations or utterances around the languages of minorities by nationalists. More often than not, they speak or write about the language(s) they belong to, which happen to be the dominant language of the region concerned, be it Telugu, Kannada, Assamese, Marathi, or others. This also allows us to notice that there are none from the communities who speak these minor languages speaking and writing about them. This only makes it evident how even during the heights of language-based movements in India, people belonging to communities that spoke 'smaller' languages were nowhere close to the bilingual nationalist elites, nor were they imagined as belonging to the 'larger' linguistic nationalist groups, or they were simply ignored. It is also here that Ambedkar's complex engagement with nationalism that argues for a nationalism sans casteism bringing people together, using a 'consciousness of kind' (Ambedkar 2002, 461–463) enabled by language among other features, helps us comprehend the minoritized's complicated negotiation with the colonizer.

There are two kinds of languages discussed in this chapter. Most of these languages addressed by the colonial apparatus, be it Toda, Badaga, Santali, Kodava, Yerava, and so on, were associated with peoples whose knowledge base revolved around small-scale agriculture, hunting, and gathering and thus not requiring the knowledge of the written word. These have primarily remained oral languages. The other set of languages that are of concern to the nationalists have been scripted, even if the written was accessible only to a very small percentage of the upper-caste males. Not only are these languages scripted and printed, but also lay claim to a long, cherished literary history and culture. My attempt here is to examine how orality has largely been constructed against the binaries of script and print. In doing so, my effort will be to map how these binaries play into further binaries where orality is relegated to the private, to the realm of tradition especially of the marginal, to that of minor languages, and to the sphere of what is construed as feminine. Whereas script and print in this process become associated with the public, with that of modern (and interestingly classical), to that of dominant languages associated with state power, with high-caste knowledge, with documented literary history, and with that of masculine—all which denote privileged domains of knowledge in today's world. Most 'minor' languages of the world remain in the sphere of the private, within the confines of the community that speaks it, yet to be 'reformed', in the very frameworks where desirable reforms for women were and are sought. While there has been a strong tendency to see script as an essential feature of the language, many Europeans have also valorized the oral traditions of these communities and many nationalists have also campaigned for a language that reaches all. What are the implications of the contradictions that at once see certain languages and orality as undesirable and as expressing the 'purest' sentiments of folk, and as something that is seen as essential to an imagined democracy are questions that I seek to analyse.

## The Nationalist Elite and Language Politic

Familiar as we are with the debates between the orientalists and the vernacularists, what often does not appear in the discourse is the debate within and among vernacularists. Indeed, as we shall see later, not all Europeans argued for a pure, standardized vernacular, whereas Assamese, Bengalis, Kannada speakers, and Telugu speakers and speakers of other major languages of India argued for a standardized, at times a pure language and at times for a language that reflected their own regional, caste, religious, and cultural locations. In her *Mysore Modern,* using the arguments made by Kannada bilingual nationalist elites, Janaki Nair shows how despite a strong presence of Islam, especially in the northern parts of Karnataka, the languages that represent Islam's past and contemporary heritage were kept behind in a narrative that favoured a particular variety of Kannada nationalism. Language, in nationalist aspirations, she argues, does not operate on its own but is enmeshed inseparably with ideas of development, religion, and caste as is the case of D. V. Gundappa who in his 1944 address says:

There are important tasks [t]hat must be undertaken for the welfare of Kannada. 1. [Both] the population of Kannadigas and the Kannada country must be expanded ... 2. Secondly, the governments of Kannada speaking regions must adopt Kannada as their own ... [i.e. make it official]. (Gundappa 2011: 247 quoted in Nair)

This leads us to the inevitable question as to who is counted as a Kannadiga and on what grounds? As Nair further argues, Kannada nationalists 'laid claim to language as a precious cultural object, a form of self-definition against outsiders within the state and not as a vehicle of democracy' (Nair 2011, 249). This meant Urdu and Hindustani and Persian, languages belonging to the spoken and literary heritage of Islam that has a strong presence in northern parts of what is now Karnataka did not belong to this realm of Kannada nationalism, not to mention other languages of minority. Different arguments for a Kannada-speaking state put forward different positions ranging from being inclusive of development, caste groups, tongues other than Kannada, and other minorities. But the love for Kannada, the basis for the argument for a *mannina maga* (son of the soil) and *Karnatakatwa* (that Aluru Venkatarao coined in 1917 describing 'the politics, dharma, history and art' of Karnataka) loomed large and was the bottom line of all positions urging for a Kannada-speaking state. As Nair posits in another essay, this love for Kannada showcases the 'Unmistakably Hindu pride', a pride that can only be afforded by caste Hindus who possess a cultural capital of written literary history among other things.

The existence of a rich literary tradition, and the output of hitherto suppressed groups such as Dalits and women, have ensured Kannada a secure place as a literary language. Yet, this domain has too has long borne the marks of hierarchy, given the extremely unequal terms of distribution of linguistic capital between the various segments of the cultural community. (Nair 1996, 2811)

To this we need to add other minorities be it Yerava, Kuruba, Kodava, and Tulu, whose cultural histories and cultural capital could not figure in the imagined nation filled with Kannadaness. In what D. R. Nagaraj classifies as 'spiritual nationalism' of Aluru Venkatarao that is seen as more accommodative than M. Chidanandamurthy's[1] 'anxiety-centric nationalism', driven by a fear of 'others', we have a variety of nationalisms in which an equal democratic space for all is largely absent. This idea of a democratic, equal space is envisioned only in recent times by very few writers among whom the most well-known is Lankesh (Nagaraj 2012, 217). Quoting Aluru's 1917 speech: 'Just as Columbus searched and dug out America, I had to search for Karnataka anew. I thought hard and studied long to find it' (Nagaraj 2012, 220–221), Nagaraj makes a very valid observation as to how the birth of all nationalisms requires a conscious effort. Alur Venkatarao, one of the doyens of Kannada nationalism, wrote his *Karnataka Gata Vaibhava* (*Karnataka's Glorious History of the Past*, 1919) using writings by the orientalists that focused on Hampi and other empires and places essentially overlapping the Hindu and Kannada identity (Venkatarao 2003, 113). With examples from the nineteenth-century Kannada Sufi traditions, missionary activities in Karnataka, and other literary traditions, D. R. Nagaraj shows how Kannada was shaped by varied traditions of Islamic and Christian practices thereby debunking any argument for a pure nationalism, linguistic or otherwise.

B.M. Srikantia, a teacher of English in the early twentieth century and a public intellectual in Kannada with a huge influence, spoke of a new Kannada in his speech given at Vidyavardhaka Sangha in Dharwad in 1911). Tharakeshwar analyses this in detail and shows how Srikantia clearly rejected the nationalist argument for having a single language for the whole of India and was not for English to be used by all. But, according to Srikantia, English was necessary to deal with the English. What is interesting is that with regard to the language of education for children, women, and Okkaligas (who are also called Gowdas, and can be classified as Shudras) in a given region (he uses the word *prantya*), Srikantia proposed the use of respective native languages (quoted in Tharakeshwar 2003, 121). What this makes very clear is that the bilingual nationalist elite constituted exclusively of upper-caste male, a refined, educated upper-caste male for whom it was necessary to be proficient in English and in his language, most likely in the standardized version, while it was sufficient for the 'others' to be educated in their 'native' languages.

---

[1] A very well-known Kannada writer and historian.

Even within the same language, there are no similarities in its usage and it is defined by the people who use it, often marked by caste is what can be gleaned by the differentiation in its use for different functions by different people. Srikantia's notion of a new Kannada, although aimed at a middle path, could not but avoid the connection between language, caste, and class. In his words, there are three varieties of Kannada:

> 1. The old one: Mainly used in books and very rule bound. 2. The one in use: Sometimes spoken in a new way though rule bound. 3. Rustic language (*gramya*): Though spoken by many people, has no rules, is lacking in knowledge, is spoken in a hurry without much attention—in use in a few regions, used mostly by lower castes and a few upper castes. (quoted in Tharakeshwar 2003, 123)

Even as these 'visionaries' imagined a new Kannada, thereby imagining a new people, a new nation of Kannada region within another imagined Indian nation, this imagination had little to do with an understanding of inequality among people by many elites of the early twentieth century. In fact, these inequalities were manifest and reinforced in their articulations on language, making language a category of not just nation building but also a category that in many ways consolidated existing hierarchies in newer ways. Sudipta Kaviraj's understanding of a categorized, stratified language and stratified society is of use here. He observes that:

> People 'having' the same language do not have it in the same way. Socially, linguistic competence confers on people capacities, and their absence correspondingly takes them away. Being Bengali is an identity coming out of a person's having the Bengali language; but clearly, all Bengalis do not have this language in the same way or to the same extent. Thus, they enjoy the political 'rights' of Bengaliness to a patently unequal degree: for some rights stemming from Bengaliness must be indivisible, but others are unequal and stratified. (Kaviraj 2010, 128)

Continuing with Bengal, we see that during the late nineteenth-century and early twentieth-century Bengal, 'the new "refined" Bengali became the hallmark of the *bhadralok* (literally, gentlefolk) or urban educated middle classes'. Anindita Ghosh writes how for those prescribing such codes of gentility, the written word became an essential tool for ordering power relations in the cultural sphere (Ghosh 2006, 5). Similar to the idea of Kannadaness that rested on a glorious literary history of the past, Ghosh draws from the manner in which European nations standardized and nationalized their language literatures and points to how these debates reflected in the discourse on civilization, which became a 'largely linguistic concept' (Ghosh 2006, 7). The written word symbolized not just the *bhadralok* but also the assertion of man's masculinity and a control over 'uneducated', basically people of lowered castes and this can be best understood by Bankim's writing in 1873:

> When readership expands, individuals from the ranks of the 'well educated' or *susikshita* and refined, step forward to educate them [less educated]. They are patronized by the larger community of the educated, and with their support, establish control over the uneducated. (Bankim 1873, 91)

If purity meant caste and guarding the refined culture patronized by the upper castes and continued control over the 'uneducated', it also meant purging of 'foreign' from one's own tongue as one can notice in the case of Telugu and Tamil. The *tanitamil* project was not just concerned with cleansing Tamil but as Sumathy Ramaswamy notes, concerns also with singularizing and homogenizing the subjectivity of its speakers, for ultimately, it is only the speaker of pure Tamil who was worthy of being called a Tamilian (Ramaswamy 1997, 154). Alongside these notions of pure and correct language practice, ideas on how a language and its history needs to be understood are also manifest. Ramaswamy's work maps the question that the Tamil nationalist Suryanarayana Sastri asked in 1903:

> 'What is the history of a language?' who then replied himself: 'the emergence of sounds to express thought and the formation of words; speech and its development into language; alphabets and their use in writing; grammatical conventions and language formation; word conventions and textual traditions—these are the contents of the history of a language. (quoted in Ramaswamy 1997, 12)

What we have here is a very linear understanding of progression. By this understanding, not only do languages that have traditions other than textual get erased from existing as languages but also the languages of the oppressed castes, labelled as dialects, whose presence in the texts is even today impossible—do not get to be languages. Added to this is the knowledge of people like Sastri who are sure that these kinds of invented histories for languages can only be constructed by people like him, thereby laying a claim over 'their' language'. The relationship of such nationalist–linguist pride to that of the oppressed castes and to women of almost all castes, who lay outside the production of such written textual knowledge, was a differentiated space within the same language which they spoke, but could not access it in its written form. This relationship needs a more nuanced understanding of Tamil *parru*,[2] the idea of devotion that made Tamil nationalism vibrant. The hierarchies that marked Tamil *parru* or Telugu *abhimanam*[3] need to be addressed at levels that marked these languages as different from the languages and people around them and not just differentiate them by positing against the languages of colonial and global order. If for Tamil, it meant cleansing Tamil of Sanskrit, for Telugu, the idea of foreign underwent a change based NOT on 'intelligibility but solely upon origins' as argued by Lisa Mitchell (2009, 124).

Ramaswamy continues to point out that these language purification movements are rarely concerned with language alone. Instead, they are crucially intertwined with questions of identity, of definitions of self and other (1997, 147). This further points to the inconsistencies prevalent around language ideology. How can we think of the attempts of nationalist elites to standardize and purify a language as homogenizing? The subjectivity of a pure Tamil can never be homogenized because the realm of purity was circumscribed by caste. The question to ask is—can a Dalit woman be a pure Tamilian? We just have to look at Bhandarkar's[4] idea of purity and language in the context of Marathi to see how elite nationalists viewed the idea of language purity and castes.

---

[2] Sumathy Ramaswamy builds on the idea of Tamil pride and devotion using this Tamil word *parru*.

[3] Similar to the above, *abhimanam* is a Telugu term is used by Lisa Mitchell.

[4] Ramakrishna Gopal Bhandarkar is known to be one of the first Indians who pioneered Indology.

We have the clearest possible evidence that Sanskrit was the vernacular of holy or respectable Brahmins of Aryavarta or North India, and who could speak this language without the study of grammar. ... Who is it that speaks good or correct Marathi? Of course Brahmins of culture. The language of other classes is not correct Marathi. The word 'sista' may be translated as 'a man of culture and education', and this education has since remote times been almost confined to Brahmins. Thus the dialects of the inscriptions of Asoka and Pali were the vernaculars of the non-Brahmanic classes; but a greater importance must evidently have been attached to them in the times of Asoka than is now assigned to the Marathi of the non-Brahmanic classes, since they are used in the inscriptions. They are, however, not recognised as independent grammarians who treated them as we treat the Marathi of the lower classes; but they were in use and bore the same relation to Sanskrit that low Marathi does to high Marathi. (quoted in Naregal 2001, 49–50)

Veena Naregal further argues how the colonial bilingual elites' 'philological valorisation of claims of purity and noble descent enabled their claims to cultivation and moral superiority in the present to be grounded in their now "proven" record as custodians of "correct" linguistic and moral practice in the past' (48). This very linear understanding and notion of positing people in a hierarchical relationship based on what they speak is a clear indication of people and language being interconnected. The conscious othering of communities happens through a conflation of caste onto language, caste purity onto language purity is a kind of hybridization that Baumann and Briggs talk about.

The poetics of otherness, at the same time it provides for oppositional contracts between others and moderns, also lays the ground for two broadly hybridising processes, one founded on cultural relativism, the other on vernacularization. (Baumann and Briggs 2003, 14–15)

Cultural relativism, a process that makes 'different' or 'alien' worlds and its people legible, works on a premise of somewhat equal worlds. But the process of vernacularization that elevates a particular variety of spoken language through the powered processes of writing. This process of otherness serves to reconfirm and reinforce existing strategies of otherness, devoid of all poetics.

These debates around various languages emerge from a variety of positions. If some in the Kannada sphere was focused on other languages that inhabited around it and not necessarily against a nationalist, anticolonial position, the debate in Bangla during the colonial period posit it as a superior language by the nationalist elite in an attempt to counter the colonial position. But, simultaneously these languages take on a colonial position in relation to other languages around them. This template of infinite reproduction of hierarchies is a factor that most language studies in India need to account for. In his "'Tongue has no bone', Bodhisattva Kar points out how the Assamese elite arguing for a distinct Assamese language and identity as against Bangla, thought of the hill languages and people in the very same manner they were up against.

> By language we understand the verbal communication of humans only, and to be specific, of only a higher class of humans … we do not honor the tongues of the undeveloped hill people and the lower classes by the name of language [*bhasha*], we call it dialect. (quoted in Kar 2008, 69)

Language becomes an honour that can only be bestowed upon a higher class of humans. The people of the hills, undeveloped, unlike the 'developed' class or caste, are not just 'lesser' human, but they are peripheral people on the hills, belong to the hills, not to civilization. Their language by implication is closer to the 'creatures' of the hills than to the civilized people of the plains. Neog's idea of 'lower' people and their 'lower' languages are very close to Srikantia's idea of languages spoken by women and Shudras and Bandarkar's idea of a language whose purity lay with certain castes. The sociopolitical power the upper castes exercised thus far and the anxiety created by the colonizer who usurped that power to some extent seems to play out in this race for continuities in power. But, to every one of these nationalists who sought to retain a caste control via purity, there is an equal counter through an ideology and practice from among the same nationalist class of educated Indian elite who used language as a democratic tool that functioned in ways thus far unimagined in caste memory. In a detailed study of modernization of spoken Telugu, known as Spoken Telugu Movement (STM), Manohar Reddy charts the various paths that Telugu modernization undertook. The growing print capitalism, the anxieties of maintaining a traditional (pure), Brahmin-based knowledge, questioning of such caste-based social practices, the entry of non-Brahmins in the field of knowledge production, the change in the economy, movement for democratizing language and society, an argument for spoken Telugu that would be accessible by everyone—all these figured prominently in STM.

In the Telugu contexts, Reddy shows us, reformists like G. Ramamurti and G. V. Appa Rao saw reform of the society as closely connected to a reform in the language used. G. V. Appa Rao, one of the foremost modern writers and activists in Telugu, talked about this connection as early as 1914. 'There is now a revolution in social and literary ideas, which will not permit the new literary language becoming the property of a learned priestly class' (140). A new language had to be wrestled from the clutches of the priestly class and caste but is also required to be wrestled from an archaic use that was alienated from the commoners, an idea which Ramamurti, the early twentieth-century Telugu reformist saw too clearly.

> As in England, so in France and America the language of books is approximated to the language current among the educated people ... But in India the birthright of the people to acquire knowledge through their own familiar language is not fully recognized [ ... ]. (quoted in Reddy 2015, 143)

In the case of Telugu, as Manohar Reddy argues, this was not merely a push towards the use of a language that was familiar to the masses but also in a manner where language could carry knowledge that was denied to the majority. 'The linguistic reform was deeply connected with the political project of social reform that the Spoken Telugu Movement undertook. Social reform [ ... ] was conceived as a constitutive element of a bigger political project: the creation of a modern society conducive to democracy' (Reddy 2015, 144–145). How across continents one can draw parallels between languages standardized and legitimized using education is perhaps best illustrated by Bourdieu with the example of French. There were also reformists like Sayyad Rahimatulla who began one of the earliest journals in Telugu despite not being a scholar of Telugu with the only intention of befriending the Hindus. This could be seen as an early recognition of the power of language in binding people together (Reddy 10–18). But there are also people like Sitaramacharyulu, who argued that 'Sanskrit was the source of all other Indian languages and insisted that, for anyone who wanted to acquire knowledge in Telugu, knowledge of Sanskrit and Prakrit was essential' (110), a factor that even today shapes official, textual, political, and institutionalized languages.

This notion of Sanskrit's centrality was clearly not accepted in the same manner among others like Ramamurti and Appa Rao. Certain reformists of the Malayalam language for example, clearly saw the impediment to the growth of language in its entrenched relation with caste and Sanskrit. K. Niveditha draws from the work of George Mattan from the late nineteenth century who wrote:

> The ancient literati of the country, being chiefly Brahmins, were only anxious to acquire a knowledge of the Sanscrit and regarded the vernacular as unworthy of their attention; which fully accounts for the want of any grammatical works by the natives themselves. (quoted in Niveditha K. 2018, 121)

Govindapillai's 1881 book *Malayala Bhasha Charitam* (*The History of Malayalam Language*) states the following as the major hindrances for the limited progress in the Malayalam language: a) the ban imposed by the Brahmins against the gaining of literacy by Shudras; and b) the reluctance on the part of ancient Rajas in patronizing local scholarly efforts at devising granthams (books) in Swabhasha; c) the attack by Tippu Sultan in AD 1788 (Niveditha 2018, 128). These varied discourses around languages inevitably address caste, either supporting the claim of purity or questioning and moving beyond the caste, language-purity claim.

E. V. Ramaswami or Periyar as he is known, represented Tamil as a worldly object and not in any divine terms. Periyar did not mince any words or thoughts in his critique of Brahminism and imposition of Hindi. Neither was he a nationalist of any sort, Tamil, Dravidian, or Indian. Not only did he mock the romanticization of the Tamil language, he also did not excuse the classical Tamil poets, thinkers, and saints for what he thought were their condescending views on women (R. K. Manoharan).[5] For Periyar, as Ramaswamy lays out, the greatness of a language rests:

> in the ease with which one could express thoughts in and through it, and the efficiency with which one could learn it; its usefulness lay in its appropriateness for any community's conditions for existence, its compatibility with the environment, and so on [ ... ]. (Ramaswamy 1997, 235)

A similar view emerges from Gandhi's understanding of language. Both Gandhi and Periyar can be said to have pushed for an idea of language as 'communicative ethos'. 'Let our chair be a *kursi*, let's not make it a *chatushpaadpeeth*' (Gandhi 1947, 45). Analysing Gandhi's views on a language that can possibly act as a binding force amongst a diverse group that was a nation in the making, Himanshu Upadhyaya notes that Gandhi 'had hoped to conserve the communicative ethos by articulating his project in conversation with an emerging Hindi movement that laid emphasis on the Nagari script. He hoped to persuade it out of business by making his preference for Hindustani known' (Upadhyaya 2010, 28). Further, Gandhi did not emphasize a language that was circumscribed by religion. He found no basis for differentiating Hindustani and Hindi. 'The language becomes Hindi when written in Devnagari and Urdu when written in Arabic ... One who is meticulous about using Sanskrit or Perso-Arabic vocabulary in one's speech only does harm to the nation' (Upadhyaya 2010, 28–29).

This strategic use of language is also true for the earliest anti-caste reformers we know during the colonial period, Jotirao Phule. He begins his *Slavery* by observing that 'the affinity existing between the Zend, the Persian and Sanskrit languages, as also between all the European languages, unmistakably points to a common source of origin' (Phule 1973, 3). Phule very convincingly and strategically used contemporary research on the history, archaeology, and philological streams to prove his point that the marauding Aryan race usurped earlier existing languages and peoples. Analysing Phule, Veena Naregal argues:

---

[5] R. M. Karthik, *Radical Freedom: Periyar and Women.* https://open-research-europe.ec.eur opa.eu/articles/1-6/v1

Phule linked it with his principal claim that Aryan ascendancy had been mainly established through the textual control that Brahmins had exercised down the ages in order to make 'pernicious legends and laws' through which they had successfully deluded and subjugated 'ignorant masses'. In this way, Phule cleverly attempted to insert lower-caste subordination into a global discourse of marginality by asserting equivalence between the subjugation of non-literate, labouring communities—across space and time—at the hands of groups who controlled inscription. (Phule 2001, 52)

Ambedkar who argued for a certain idea of a national language, argued for it because he thought language could bring about a fellow-feeling, a 'consciousness of kind' in a society like India that was riven with economic conflicts and social gradation. In one of the most perceptive understandings of the idea of the Indian nation state, he says 'it is a longing not to belong to any other group' (1995, 15). While pointing out that a linguistic state with its regional language as its official language may easily develop into an independent nationality (18), his argument for linguistic states was very clear. 'To make easy way to democracy and to remove racial and cultural tension' (17).

It is not surprising that a non-glorified view of language, a very pragmatic notion of language in practice and ideology comes from anti-caste thinkers. For them, the use of language had everything to do with an equal society, a society where everyone had access to knowledge in languages that enable and empower them. Language had to be linked to dignified livelihood practices, not to mention its use towards democracy and fraternity, the bedrocks of modern political society along with equality. Arguing for language as a political commons, Madhava Prasad says: 'Language, however, is not merely a cultural requisite for a nation-state, it is rather a morphological prerequisite of the nation-state form. Whether this requirement constitutes a limitation or a spur to emancipation is the question' (2914, 95). Further, Prasad urges us to think of 'Language is a prerequisite of the nation-state form because it alone can secure a political symbolic that is capable of limiting, if not eliminating altogether, the need for transcendent icons of political authority' (97). Do languages transcend icons of political authority? What other authorities have dominant languages brought about? The question of languages of minority within this political commons, is bound to be relegated to the role of the ethnie as he points out. But, 'the assumption of political identity by an ethnic group is achieved at the cost of the alienation of one of its attributes, language' (97) and the speakers of the minority language are compelled to learn the language of the nation state in order to participate in political life leads us to ask many questions—how do we then access this foundational commons that has to be made available for all, for sharing, for use in an equitable manner? In what ways can an Adivasi from Jharkhand access the language of political commons if not in their own language or in English to which everyone aspires? Why should the nation state be so inaccessibly (indecently) large, grand, far away, so centralized that we need a larger-than-life commons? Commons is something closer to us, which we can access, in our own language, in practices immediate to us. This nationalist idea of democracy that feels the need of a commons in the language a nation functions, hardly recognizes the commons as endowed with a class and caste prestige. What needs to be noted is that there is nothing to stop languages in the plural to operate in the commons, especially when we understand politics as inseparable from our daily lives.

## The Colonizer, Administrator, Missionary: Also the Linguist

As we saw, the nationalist elites represented languages and the people who spoke them in ways that are complex and brought to the fore notions of caste and anti-caste; and notions of maintaining a status quo with an idea of pure language. There were also representations of language as communicative, as reaching out to allincluding languages being inclusive and of exclusive. Similarly, representations of languages by the colonizer also come across as equally complex. Was there a singular notion of civilization? Were 'exotic' languages seen as primitive? Were people who spoke languages but did not use the writing system seen as undeveloped? How did the colonizer with the written letter construe languages that did not belong to him[6] but was keen to know, and perhaps control? It is not

---

[6] It is unsurprising that all scholars/administrators mentioned here, be it nationalist or colonialist, are men.

just in the realm of understanding the languages that the colonizer and missionary made a mark. It is well known that the languages of India, although only the major ones, which the colonizers considered worthy, were institutionalized mainly during the colonial period. This had ripple effects like that in Assam where Bangla, the official language for a long time got to be contested and went through a movement. Thanks to the unintentional collaboration between the printing presses, caste elites, missionaries, and colonial machineries, alongside production of text books, magazines, newspapers, literary texts, and pamphlets that aided in the processes of vernacularizations, languages were also institutionalized through other means. In detailing how languages like Kannada entered the institutional realm, Tharakeshwar notes a known fact as to how money that came to the British government after the fourth Anglo-Mysore War was utilized to teach native languages. The Fort Williams College was established using this money where at first the North Indian languages were given priority along with the teaching of Hindu religious texts. Later, South Indian languages were included in the curriculum (Tharakeshwar 2003, 94). If institutionalizing meant formal teaching and learning activities, for our purposes it also means production of a discourse in the public domain. This discourse combined with other discourses, brought the languages of the minorities to the fore as never before.

One of the earliest linguists who worked on lesser known languages of India, M. B. Emeneau, puts things in perspective and asserts how these 'small' languages hold their own:

> The languages of the Bergies is a dialect of the Canarese; that of Todevies and Kotis is supposed to be a dialect of the Tamil. But it is a singular fact that the Todevies cannot speak the language of the Kotis, or the Kotis that of the Todevies, and the language of both these classes is equally unintelligible to the Bergies. (1994a, 387)

That despite the familial connection, these languages are languages in their own right is something that linguists like Emeneau have held since the early twentieth century, an aspect that dominant nationalist aspirations have at best tried to ignore.

Contradictions are true for the most famous of all linguists among the colonial administrators South Asia has known, G. A. Grierson. Rita Kothari charts the manner in which Grierson identified and named the languages as distinct, and creating new sensibilities of the idea of belonging. Grierson's work also led to ideas that distinguished languages from dialects. Grierson uses the example of Jangali, a language spoken in some regions in Punjab to discuss how 'The average Indian villager does not know that he has been speaking anything with a name attached to it. He can always put a name to the dialect spoken by somebody fifty miles off [ … ]' (Grierson 1927, 19). Whether the person wants to answer the question asked, and whether the person wishes to identify the language in the manner sought by the interviewer, whether notions of identity and language are intertwined with other categories like caste, region, community, and how the average villager perceives the role of language in their day-to-day lives and connects them to the larger realms, are questions that we need to ask.

What is significant for us in this debate is how languages like Assamese whose protagonists saw as being subsumed by Bengali got a new lease of life by such studies claiming a distinct nationality for languages. For Grierson, the criteria for a nationality that could be claimed as separate was its distinct written literature and history. While we will discuss later Grierson's views on languages that were oral in nature which took an altogether different tangent; languages like Assamese that are written but were not yet mainstream like that of Bengali, can be said to have benefited from Grierson's assertions of a separate nationalist identity. In his review of Javed Majeed's work, Tariq Rahman notes that Grierson departed from the:

> supremacist colonial position to a position that was new, and had a certain sense of autonomy of his 'subject' of study. He did not fully subscribe to such a supremacist discourse, and, in fact, on one occasion he was seen by senior officials as providing support to Indian nationalism in his work. (Rahman 2019, 70)

From what Grierson has to say about Assamese in the passage below, we can safely assume that his work indeed can be seen as supporting

nationalisms of different kinds, which coming from a colonial administrator is something.

> [Assamese] is now admitted to be an independent language, yet if
> merely its grammatical form and its vocabulary are considered, it would
> not be denied it is a dialect of Bengali. Yet its claim to be considered as
> an independent language is incontestable. Not only is the speech of an
> independent nation, with a history of its own, but it has a fine literature
> differing from that of Bengal both in its standard of speech, and in its
> nature and content. Here, therefore, we have an example of a language
> differentiated from its neighbours not by mutual unintelligibility but by
> nationality and literature. (Grierson 1927, 24)

One can notice how a language gets labelled as a language, gets its position as a language of worth, distinct from its neighbours not because it is
unintelligible to speakers of other languages in the neighbourhood, but
because it could showcase its written record, be it literature or history. It
is not just a matter of literature and history as Grierson argues, but how
these two categories are made essential to the idea of nationality is the
question worth probing. Although nationality and nationalist expressions have been expressed in writing since ancient times[7], nationality in
the last 300 years as Benedict Anderson has pointed out, has been associated mainly with writing, with print capitalism making it easier to spread
this new but dominating idea. If we consider neighbouring languages of
Bengali and Assamese such as Khasi, Garo, Bodo, Santali, and Ho, that
are so mutually unintelligible to each other and perhaps have been articulating a consciousness of community, bound by language and ethnic attributes with a territorial imagination in their oral lore, this consciousness
of community perhaps is stronger than the nationalisms that emerged in
late nineteenth and early twentieth centuries. If, then, nationality is articulated only by writing that was rediscovered and brought to the realm
of public discussion only in the nineteenth and twentieth centuries, especially in the case of many languages of India, the strategies used by
people who speak 'minor' languages in constituting an identity of their

---

[7] *Kavirajamarga* in Kannada in the ninth century is said to have imagined a Kannada nation
and so have medieval Kannada poets like Pampa.

own, their understanding of who they are, their perceptions around how others perceive them ... constitutes a huge vacuum in our understanding of nationalism. Grierson's complex subject position, as Tariq Rahman argues, can be understood by locating him as a 'cross-border' figure: [who] came from Anglo-Irish roots and therefore brought with him strong perceptions of nationality for different people, playing a major role in giving prominence to linguistic and regional identities.

Interesting can be an understatement when it comes to the studies and statements made by colonizers on languages of India, whether dominant or of minorities. Sir Arthur Cotton, the well-known irrigation engineer and British general known for the bridges he built also wrote *A Study of Living Languages* in 1857.

> The learning of the living languages of foreign, semi-civilized and savage people has now become a matter of such immeasurable importance that any man may be excused who makes the poorest attempt to diminish the difficulties of such a work. [ ... ] This is in some important respects quite distinct from both the acquisition of dead languages of nations who have been fully civilized and, consequently have a complete system of literature, a great variety of books of instruction written by extensively informed natives, and also thoroughly educated teachers. (Arthur Cotton 1857, i and ii)

In one single paragraph, we have a plethora of ideas. How and why is the association of living languages made with foreign, semi-civilized, savage people, alongside the claim that learning such languages is not easy at all. How can savage people be capable of such complexities that are incomprehensible to the knowledgeable and civilized? While there are informed teachers and a great variety of books to learn the dead languages, there exists no such system to learn these living languages. The term 'living' in itself is interesting. Does this mean that English and other languages are not living languages? Does this mean civilized societies are at a dead end? By living does Cotton mean spoken and not existing only in written like in Latin or Sanskrit? Or does Cotton mean these languages inhabit people and their worlds unlike the language of the books which do not connect to most people? Does Cotton mean that taking pride in being civilized does not matter since it is already dead? Civilization leads to death? That it is the 'savage' that lives and thrives? What I want to note here is that construction of the communities emerges as a construction that complicates an essentialized identity. We see that these binaries of dead and civilized, living and uncivilized operate in a very interesting way in relation to—the concept of the noble savage being a category constructed in eighteenth- and nineteenth-century Europe.[8] How do we understand this? Can we attribute other meanings to the word 'savage' other than the usual colonial ones?

Charles Gover, a British administrator and folklorist, wrote a good number of articles and compiled a book on the South Indian languages. He held the belief that all Dravidian, i.e. South Indian languages were Aryan in origin. In 1871, he complied the *Folk Songs of Southern India*, in which many of his observations are worthy of mention.

> They are for the most part peoples without a literature and without a history. But, it will be seen that the Dravidian peoples possess one of the noblest literatures, from a moral point of view, the world has seen. (Gover 1871, viii)

There is a 'but' that Gover inserts in his above statement. People without a written literature and without a written history are not necessarily immoral, they are definitely not primitive from positions of the high morality held by Victorian white men or Brahmin men. How does Gover go on to prove this? By using the folklore of the people in most parts of the Dravidian speaking world. It is this oral folklore that establishes the noble nature of these people, in fact these are the noblest literatures. Gover did not just compile the oral literature of the major Dravidian languages but also included Badaga and Coorg songs within the book.

For Gover, the idea that peoples without literature and without history stand tall morally—is at once Christian, at once patronizing but also elevating the people on a platform that does not judge based on writing and history proper. Although the claim 'without' is a negating category of sorts, the implications move beyond negation to an identity built on particular values, even if it seems Christian. It is the people with their living songs, tales that are told, and lives that are lived that matter, not the

---

[8] See *The Dawn of Everything* for more details.

word on the page that is counted as history. It is here perhaps that people like Gover and Cotton unconsciously posit certain values in utterances, in speech acts, and performative acts of languages. These languages that did not 'record' their literature or history in writing did not have a specialized role in the public. They were indeed living a life that belonged to the land and people they were part of, and by recording and recognizing such languages and peoples, Gover, Cotton, and others would only encourage, enable people who spoke such languages even if they could not perhaps access or manage to read what was written about them. In stark contrast to many others, colonizers and native nationalists, who wrote about 'unlettered' hill people as 'low', here are accounts that perceive them altogether differently.

In addition, another significant observation is made by Grierson in relation to the difference in the written and the spoken form of the same language.

> The best known Dravidian languages are Tamil, Malayalam, Kanarese, and Telugu. They have all for a long time been used as literary languages. Their literature is, in the case of all of them, written in a language which differs more or less from every-day speech, and is usually recognized as a separate dialect. (1906: 282)

Curiously and correctly, the written form is also termed as a dialect of the language. It is here that the caste question comes in, urging us to ask why exactly the written dialect is different from the spoken one. Questions as to who writes and what makes that writing valid and how is this construed as legitimate written knowledge, keeping the distinctions between written and spoken distinct and clear need attention. These questions as mentioned cannot but be analysed from the framework of caste. This differentiation between written and the spoken also maintains a distinction between the upper-caste male who wrote, standardizing the language with the knowledge of Sanskrit *he had* and the upper-caste women and persons of lowered castes who spoke the languages in the forms familiar to them. This difference that continues to this day between the spoken and written, official and uttered, institutionalized and practised at home, even as it is done within the ambit of the same language is what makes difficult Madhava Prasad's idea of 'language as Political Commons'. While

Prasad argues that a certain Political Commons essential for the working of a democracy is possible only through a language commons, Le Page points to the contradictions inherent in this assumption.

> From a vantage point in Western Europe or North America, it might appear as if democracy could not possibly work unless these conditions were satisfied; with an elected government passing laws in a language which the people could understand, so that they could discuss them. [...] True democracy in the sense of a continuing dialogue between people and their elected representatives in the Government can only really be achieved in small homogenous tribal societies. (Le Page 2020, 530)

Bishop Robert Caldwell (whom Grierson dutifully follows), a missionary who believed in the teachings of the Bible in the native language, is now known for his *The Comparative Grammar of South Indian Languages*. Caldwell's work moved towards classifying languages into dialect and language, and dialects as corrupt versions of languages. But as we shall notice, there are instances where these classifications are blurred, often confusing the reader. As one can see from the quote from Caldwell, the languages perceived as cultivated are 'not mere provincial dialects' but are uncultivated 'idioms' like the Dravidian 'idioms'.

> The various Dravidian idioms, though sprung from a common origin, are (therefore) to be considered not as mere provincial dialects of the same speech, but as distinct though affiliated languages. They are as distinct one from the other as Spanish from Italian, Hebrew from Aramaic, Sindhi from Bengali [ ... ] The uncultivated idioms Tuda, Kota, Gond, Khond and the Oraon must differ still more widely both from one another and from the cultivated languages. (Caldwell 1875, 44–45)

What is interesting is that the Dravidian idioms are compared with Spanish, or Italian. They might be neighbouring, might have sprung from the same origin, but they are distinct. In fact, the smaller Dravidian tongues not only differ from one another, but also differ widely from the 'cultivated' ones, by which we can safely assume the ones that have a written version of the language. It is the aspect of mutual intelligibility that framed the idea of a language for Caldwell. This is a criteria that made these languages 'language' per se and the concepts of 'idiom', 'dialect', and 'language' are interchangeable and seem constantly fluctuating. It is through such discourses, I argue, that languages which remained in their specific region, their function and role limited to specific communities, moved beyond their locale, even if notionally, and acquired an identity, got connected with a larger discourse via a new discourse, albeit colonial. 'Tuda, Kota, Gond, and Kui, though rude and uncultivated, are undoubtedly to be regarded as essentially Dravidian dialects, equally with the Tamil, the Canarese and the Telugu' (Caldwell 40). For Caldwell here, rude and uncultivated notwithstanding, there was nothing 'material' to rank the languages of minority lower than that of the written/cultivated ones.

An unlettered language in effect is a language that lives and sustains in its oral self. How did the colonizer translate this notion of orality into their systems of writing? G. Richter, a missionary based in Coorg, R. A. Cole, an administrator, and Moegling, another missionary, attempt to establish an affinity between Kodava and the major Dravidian languages while simultaneously maintaining a difference. Richter says: 'The Kodagu language is shorter, more simple, but less refined than the Canarese and a convenient medium for conversation. The Kodavas have a language of their own which is intelligible only to themselves' (Richter 1870, 193–194). This is important because a language belonging to a small number of people is not dismissed as a dialect or as an unrefined form of a major language.

Attempts in writing grammar also produced interesting results. One of the main things I noticed is how R. A. Cole lists fourteen vowels, twenty-five classified consonants, and nine unclassified consonants including aspirated consonants for Kodava. Richter, writing thirteen years after Cole, reduced the number of Kodava letters in the alphabet by deleting the aspirated consonants, much like the tradition in Tamil, thereby deleting the Sanskrit infusion of aspiration in the written tradition. This is also an indication of how Richter saw the closely connected Dravidian tongues but also argued for the conversational suitability of Kodava that did not require aspiration. While this effort can be understood as an attempt to classify languages that were different from the aspirated Indo-Aryan languages it can also be seen as simultaneously forging an affinity among the Dravidian while also 'giving' languages like Kodava 'a grammar of their own'.

One of the major ways in which many languages are judged and classified is by the presence of a long written literary history as opposed to a history of orality. For Richter, 'Strictly speaking, there is no literature in the Kodagu language, as a few indigenous songs of a very limited range of subjects compromise the whole catalogue' (1870, 208). This is the very same notion that is carried over by Bishop and Caldwell. In fact, Caldwell who wrote a comparative grammar of Dravidian languages lists the cultivated languages of South India as Tamil, Canarese, Telugu, and Canarese and adds Tulu and Kodava as two languages which he has doubts about adding to this list of cultivated languages.

> But though I have thought it best to give this language a place amongst the cultivated members of the family, the propriety of doing so seems to me still more doubtful than that of placing Tulu in this list. In the first edition of this work, this language was not assigned to it a place of its own, but was included under the head of Canarese. It had been generally considered rather as an uncultivated dialect of Canarese, modified by Tulu, rather than as a distinct language. (Caldwell 1875, 36)

What baffles me is this: Bishop Caldwell's mission as well as that of other grammarians in the period was to establish a strong connection among the Dravidian languages and they succeeded in doing so. Even as the relationships between Tamil, Canarese, Telugu, and Malayalam was so very strong and evident in their connection, they were classified as separate, as cultivated, as developed. While Kodava's or Tulu's connection to these languages made them only subordinate, not otherwise. This I argue is an assumption derived from the presence of written cultures.

Grierson, too, posits an assumption that can throw a different insight into the connections between race, language, and people. 'It is also probable that the Tribes who speak the various broken dialects in Western India, such as Kols, and so forth, have originally used a Munda form of speech. On the other hand, several Aryanized Tribes of Northern India have certainly once spoken some Munda dialect' (1906, 9).

Grierson's accounts are questionable on many accounts. Not only are 'small' languages associated with 'small' groups of people termed as broken dialects, there is an assumption of Aryanization as a one-way movement of languages and people. But observations such as the above showcase how it is the Mundari languages that can claim an ancient past and not the much celebrated Indo-Aryan languages, mainly Sanskrit. It is the Mundari that the Aryan languages replaced and therefore it is the Mundari languages that are older than the Aryan one. Recent studies (Tony Joseph, 2018 and Peggy Mohan, 2021), have pointed out how different waves of migration into the Indian subcontinent have altered the language-scape and how Indo-Aryans were perhaps the last to arrive. Although this knowledge was not available to Grierson, in a context where Sanskrit was touted as the national sacred, the mention of how people and tribes who use Indo-Aryan languages once perhaps used Mundari languages, the languages of the indigenous hill people, thereby bringing into discourse a radical view that questions the very nature of nationalist continuities of particular cultures. Who are these Aryanized tribes is a question that is left unanswered.

The standard of comparison is always the 'big' language of the region and the movement between language and dialect unilinear, despite the distinction between language and dialect not very clearly described. This is also evident in Grierson's quote of Richard Temple who says: 'The Nicobarese speak one language in six dialects so different as to be mutually unintelligible to the ear' (1906, 15). Mutual intelligibility now being one of the main criteria to distinguish between language and dialects, we see that Grierson often slips into this differentiation based on the races and their numbers. He gives accounts of:

Dravidian dialects [that] properly fall within the scope of this survey, but short accounts will also be given of Tamil, Malayalam, Kanarese, and Telugu, the principal Dravidian languages of the south. The minor dialects of south India, on the other hand, such as Kodagu, Tulu, Kota will not be described. (1906, 276)

Independent India seems to have inherited this trait of not describing, and worse, not counting 'minor languages' spoken by less than 10,000 people. Grierson benevolently describes these minor languages using Caldwell's book, whose vague distinction between language and dialect Grierson used copiously.

The [Tuda] language seems to have been originally old Canarese and not a distinct dialect. A few Tamil forms were introduced by the poligars. Intercourse with the Badaga has probably modernized a few of the forms, and introduced some words. Of Telugu influences I see no trace. Nor can I trace any resemblance in Toda to Malayalam. (quoted in Grierson 1906, 283)

As mentioned, comparison is always made between a minor language and a major one. This, as critics of French School of Comparatists point out, implies an influence that is associated with power. Influence studies within the field of comparative literature and linguistics largely assume that a literature or language influenced by another is necessarily inferior. This also does not take into account the contexts in which these influences arise. Especially in the case of speech forms, where directions of influences are hard to pin down, these assumptions of a unilinear influence flowing from the big to small have continued to exist in both popular and academic perceptions.

And again, the language/dialect distinction is blurred in almost all these accounts. Dialects that are mutually unintelligible are still dialects, principal Dravidian languages are also dialects, minor dialects are also dialects, but not worthy of description. These issues only point to how the distinction between language and a dialect is not crystallized in the early twentieth century. Also, the so-called minor languages, usually spoken by Tribes and people of hills, are not always dismissed as 'dialects' as was done in 1929 by the Assamese nationalist Neog who is quoted earlier in the chapter. What is it that characterizes this difference in discourse? There is of course consolidation of colonialism by the 1920s and the knowledge that it generated through the study of 'oriental' languages and literatures over nearly a century that marked certain tongues as languages and certain others as dialects, based largely on notions of written literature and written history. Why did the nationalist elite whose ideology was diametrically opposite to that of the colonizer find it productive to use divisive, hierarchical notions when it came to people who lived in the same region as them? If the Christian idea of salvation pushed the missionaries to be benevolent, the caste idea of superiority further manifested in the realm of language as in other realms. For most nationalist elites being born to the castes considered higher, any people belonging to the lowered castes and to the hills were beyond this idea of a 'pure' identity built on the caste and a glorified view of this caste's past. Any consideration of these 'outliers' as their own, including the languages they spoke would only dent the carefully built identity. It is therefore caste and its associated notion of purity that kept people and their languages aside. One could safely argue that language was used as an easy criteria through which people whom the elite wished to exclude could be kept aside in their articulation of a particular kind of nationality and merit.

If one notices the manner in which the Yerava language of the Yerava Tribe spoken in the border areas of Kerala and Karnataka is counted, the inconsistency with which languages and dialects are marked by census is baffling. Yerava, a tribe that inhabits the Coorg/ Kodagu and Waynad districts bordering Karnataka and Kerala states of India have been at the receiving end of caste–feudal societies since the precolonial times, during colonization, and today. Many external factors have led to the tribe's gradual decrease in numbers, now less than ten thousand, leading to the census of India not counting them and the language they speak, thereby making invisible their existence. This invisiblizing happens not just through bounded categories like the census but also in abstract categories like that of an identity. Never to be identified as a tribe whose practices are and used to be self-sustainable, often the tribe and their practices including their language is subsumed or at worst erased as belonging to one of the lowest in the imagined order of humans. Grierson mentions that 'Yerava has been returned as such a form of speech (a dialect from Malayalam) from Coorg, and the figures for that dialect have, therefore, been added to those returned for Malayalam' (1906, 348).

In fact, the structured hierarchy between language and dialect seems to be a new phenomenon reinforced over time. The first ever census of India in 1871 classifies Yerava as a language. In 1881 this changes to a 'wild dialect'. In 1891 and 1901, it is written off as 'the tongue of the Tribe and as a dialect of Malayalam', The *Linguistic Survey of India* mentions Yerava to be a dialect of Malayalam. Mallikarjun's study documents how in the census of 1921, Yerava is mentioned as a 'peculiar language of Coorg', and in 1931 it becomes one of the 'principal indigenous languages of Coorg' (1993, 46). Not just that the identities of the languages and the people who speak them are officially construed in a manner that is inconsistent, unstable (as against legitimate, stable nationalist written ones), but also offensive to the people who have no means to question such constructions. Talal Asad's idea of 'languages of inequality' where not only the colonizer but also the anthropologist (postcolonial, imperial, neocolonial, or casteist) assert such classification and understanding of a people without a reflection on the power that makes such classification possible weighs heavily in the case of Yerava. Added to this is the post-independent India's practices that do not count languages whose speakers number less than ten thousand people that erases the very existence of a people who live in conditions similar to bonded slavery. In the case of Yerava, it gets erased by Kodava within the context of Kodagu (Coorg) or when we move away from the immediate locale, it is Kannada/Malayalam. In one of most perceptive observations on the relationships between languages and people, Pattabhirama Sommayyaji says:

> Kodagu's eighteen (mostly tribal) languages are attempted to be presented as deviations/dialects of the dominant languages of the surrounding region, but their numbers are only in dwindling hundreds. These Tribes have also been aggressively dispossessed politically, territorially, religiously, and culturally for at least over two centuries now. Presently, they are endangered semiotic-systems/languages/cultures/peoples. Conversely, the Kodava language, the language of the dominant minority in Kodagu, is attempting to garner aggressive political clout by demanding a place in the 8th schedule of the constitution. The situation is created/aggravated by its agitation for separate statehood. (2002, 144)

## Language, Race, Caste, and People

There are hardly any accounts of language that do not make the connection between race and people. One of the central emphasis (and uses) of philology has been to classify races and people, and accounts of languages of India are no different. Many of these accounts do see colonizers as harbingers of knowledge and as mentioned earlier, many European accounts also question the guarded written knowledge of the Brahmin caste. Interestingly, stalwarts of Indian linguistics fall right into this trap of equating language–people groups with writing as superior races. Suniti

Kumar Chatterji, one of the most known linguists from India, saw Aryan groups as the most important among linguistic and cultural groups. Further, for Chatterji: 'Indian civilisation has found its expression primarily through the Aryan speech as it developed through the centuries' (1971, 5).

If a civilization is built on the written expression of a miniscule number of people in a language that was accessible only to them, a whole lot of other languages get characterized as backward and primitive in the writings of scholars like Chatterji.

> Other languages of the Sino-Tibetan family and also of the Austric family were in a backward state, as the speakers of these were in a comparatively primitive condition in their way of life. Of course, they had some kind of village or folk culture, but no civilization. Connected with this culture there developed in all these languages a slight modicum of folk-literature—of songs, religious and otherwise, of folk-tales, and of their legends and traditions. These were never written down as they lacked any system of writing. (1971, 6)

Sino-Tibetan and Austric families of languages largely belong to the east and northeastern parts of India and are spoken by Tribes. It is here that the caste complex of mainland Indian scholarship and writing comes to the fore via characterizing what they possess as infinitely superior. Tribes by virtue of existing in the realm of folk are not part of a civilization envisioned by this caste complex. Writing is what constitutes civilization albeit the majority being left out of it. And what began with the arrival of Europeans does not really count for, as Chatterji observes, 'the modern literature which had started under European and an Christian inspiration is not as yet of any value' (1971, 8).

Even prior to Chatterji, the venerated Assamese writer and intellectual Lakshminath Bezbaroa saw people around his own location as being nowhere close to the Assamese culture he was part of: 'the languages of the Nagas, Miris, Mishmis, and similar savage people are poor, because their ideas are poor (quoted in Kar 2008, 69), basically implying a civilizational difference between the caste groups and the Tribes.

Civilization, the word as we now know and as Raymond Williams has charted, is derived from the Latin term *civilis* meaning 'of or belonging to citizens' (1976, 57). "In modern English, civilization still refers to a general condition or state, and is still contrasted with savagery or barbarism (1976, 59).

In addition, dominant understanding has almost always equated civilization with culture and a written culture at that. This understanding can be traced to early Europeans travelling through America and to early anthropologists in the late nineteenth and early to mid-twentieth centuries who used 'civilization' and 'civilized society' to differentiate between societies they found culturally superior (which they were often a part of) and those they found culturally inferior (which they referred to as 'savage' or 'barbaric' cultures). 'Walter Benjamin's often quoted words are telling here: 'There is no document of civilization which is not at the same time a document of barbarism'.[9] Telling in this context are the arguments of Graeber and Wengrow who point to the non-democratic, uncivilized nature of Europeans and to the largely peaceful and much more equal native American societies as civilized. What we have is a very complicated history that makes defining a civilization very difficult to explain.[10] But for scholars like Chatterji, civilization was a given and we can see the ramifications of these constructs in the contemporary lives and politics of people from the northeast of India.

In contrast, we also have linguists like M. B. Emeneau who said: 'It will be remembered that communities in Indian caste complexes tend to insist on their differences, both for mutual differentiation and as symbols of intra-community solidarity' (1994a, 387). To this solidarity one must add inter-community hierarchy. The differentiation here lies not just in a relativist difference but in the hierarchy that in essence cannot be bridged. Rev. Richter, a missionary in the Basel missionary in Coorg/ Kodagu, observation as to how this hierarchy plays out in the realm of language among different communities in Kodagu is telling: Kaplas, one of the Tribes in Kodagu 'imitate as much as they can the customs of their masters whose language they also use' (quoted in Rao and Lokesh 1998, 150). This language–people connection then is seen by the majority as a process akin to Sanskritization where people perceived as lower in the

---

[9] Walter Benjamin: *Concept of History*
[10] https://www.nationalgeographic.org/encyclopedia/civilizations/ and https://www.world history.org/civilization/

order and inferior, are seen as standing on uncertain grounds of their own identity and their aspiration is always towards an identity that is imitated. If there are indications and movements otherwise, they do not get recorded.

Bishop Caldwell, about whom we have read early in the chapter, urged 'natives' of South India to take an active interest in the comparative study of their own languages. For him, this interest combined with:

Comparative philology in general, [ ... ] would find it in a variety of ways much more useful to them than the study of grammar of their own language alone ever has been. I trust the interest taken in their language, literature, and antiquities by foreigners will not be without its effect in kindling amongst the natives of south India a little wholesome, friendly rivalry. (Caldwell 1875, x)

This is only a small peek into how languages are mapped to identities and rivalry. They are mapped as belonging to particular groups of people, they are also mapped as a family of connected groups of people. And this is definitely only in relation to the antiquities of the written languages.

Further for Caldwell, the languages of people who inhabit the peripheries, unlike the 'civilized' ones in the plains, are dialects that are as unworthy as the people themselves. Their illegible lives that are unperceivable by the colonizer and caste network can only find meaning in labels such as 'wandering' and 'predatory'.

These kinds of descriptions that unhesitatingly create binaries are pushed ahead in not just texts that engage with languages but also in a diverse range of texts like *Provincial Geographies*:

The nomad Lambadis, Brinjaris, or Sugalis have a language, which has been said to be usually based on one of the local vernaculars, embroidered and diversified with theives' slang and expression borrowed from the various localities in which the Tribe has sojourned. Like the Lambadis, the wandering Koravas or Yerukalas, who call their language Oodra (possibly a corruption of Odiya OR *kannada oddaru*), have a theives' slang, and call a head-constable the man who rides on an ass, a constable a red-haired man, rupees—milk eyes and so on. (1913, 124)

Uncultivated languages belong to uncultivated classes and communities. And more crucially they are 'corrupted', they are not as pure as the plains people's language or as pure as plains people themselves. The superimposition of language and a people with categories that not only stereotype but are used, conflated with people considered to be 'primitive' thereby reinforcing existing divisions. We cannot but notice that most of these people considered uncultivated, primitive, thieves are Tribes. Whether tribe as a category emerged from these philological meanderings is a question that is debated. But the fact that these groups are indigenous, autonomous, and outside the caste system, and do not self-identify with any of these negative constructions of identity categories is evident. Let us consider Grierson's observation on Korava: 'consistency cannot, of course, be expected in the dialect of a Tribe' (1906, 282). How do we understand this? That non-tribal languages are very consistent? As we saw earlier on, Grierson maintained that written classical languages like Tamil and Kannada was entirely a different dialect than that of the colloquially spoken one. Is the consistency associated with the written variety of a particular language? And since most tribal languages are speech forms, this consistency or in other words standardization cannot be expected. Or does consistency lie with a notion of purity, a language that is sanitized, cleaned of all 'vulgarities'.

What one can note is that even among the smaller languages, there is a marked difference of power of the people who speak it. Tulu speakers who are not only numerically larger than Manjhi but also exert considerable power in the region, coastal Karnataka, they inhabit (and now outside too). Manjhi, unlike Tulu, is so invisible/insignificant that it does not matter and perhaps matters to point how languages are impure and corrupt. Marking the written, which is often associated with the higher caste elites, or rather the written which was accessible to the higher caste elites is clubbed with purity. Baumann and Briggs point out how this notion of purity is gendered and also associated with aristocratic classes in the English context and in the Indian context. Anindita Ghosh and Bodhisatva Kar have argued that purity of language was a much debated issue resulting in the carving out of a standardized language that was gendered, region-based, and caste-inflected.

Quite a few writings by Europeans from the late nineteenth and early twentieth centuries recognize the autonomy and also the hierarchy among and between certain communities. Charles Gover, the folklorist who compiled *The Folk-Songs of Southern India*, said this about the mountainous Tribes and their relationship to each other:

> These hills and green plateau are the home to several moun-
> tain Tribes. The Kurgis are the highest, the Kotas the lowest in the
> tribal scale. Below the noblest are the Todas. Above the basest are
> the Badagas. Other Tribes are called Kurumbers and Irulas. They all
> speak varieties of Hali Cannadi or ancient Canarese, and doubtless
> represent, almost unchanged, the condition, speech and occupation
> of the great original stock which has progressed and become civilised
> in Mysore until it has become what we now see in the Cananrese na-
> tion. (1871, 63)

One can notice the obvious discrepancies in Gover's ideas of the elite and the mass here in the above quote and in the introduction to his book. In the introduction and even here, although Gover reserves the status of the civilized to all the Tribes, there is an evident hierarchy within the Tribes he describes. The scale on which the high and lows of civilization was measured is not clear. Throughout the book, Gover maintained that it is only through the songs of the people that one could have a knowledge of the 'inner life' of a people. This very Herderian idea of the folk that romantizes a people and its 'natural ways' of life acts as a way of under-standing people, however orientalist, as a people whose practices vary from that of the dominant Hindu around them.

Gover, in the same book, pointedly argues how this hierarchy operates in the realm of writing and how caste is at its centre.

> The editing of all books gradually fell on them, because they alone had
> the leisure and knowledge that literary labour required. The brahmans
> have corrupted what they could not destroy. Indigenous poetry fell into
> undeserved contempt or, where that was not possible, was edited so un-
> scrupulously, that the original was hidden under a load of corruption.
> (1871, 14)

Since it was largely the Brahmin whose written (or even speech forms) representations were taken to be authentically Indian, Gover takes this a little further and makes clear the connection between knowledge, religion, language, and caste.

> There seldom seem to dawn upon the mind a single suspicion that perhaps so exclusive a caste, so jealous of contact with the impure masses around, so determined to keep to itself all the religious books, so pertinacious in maintaining its own essential superiority, is not a fair representation of the masses it despises, and with whom it will have no dealings. (1871, 2)

Among the many exceptions to linear orientalist studies and representations of minor languages, M. B. Emeneau is the most perceptive. He systematically argues against particularist stereotypes of orality, of people, and the languages they speak, especially the communities that many consider 'unlettered'. By pointing out the interactions between various languages big and small, during times thought of as ancient and modern, he does not see them as a people and language fixed in a time that is not coeval. Operating outside the frame of 'imitation' and 'corrupt', he charts the interactions of languages using notions of power and the lack of it associated with communities and languages.

> There seemed to be a sort of taken for granted consensus that archaism is a 'universal' of the language of poetry, or perhaps of oral poetry. But I could not, and still cannot, find there is any definition of the corpora of which this 'universal' is predicated or of the ways in which archaism is manifested. (Emeneau 1994b, 287)

Gover too makes many a point regarding the contemporariness of orality, the everydayness and their easy accessibility. This conscious juxtaposition of commoners' poetry as against the elite written word is how these 'smaller' languages and spoken speech gained a certain momentum in the public.

> It is often been said that there is no better way of discovering the real feelings and ideas of a people than afforded by the songs that pass from lip to lip in their streets and markets. None know whence they come.

Verses are added, to or subtracted from them as new ideas come in or old ideas pass away. Thus they keep up to date, as it were, the expression of those inner feelings which never rise to the surface of a set of literature, but are in reality the very essence of popular belief. (Gover 1871, 1)

Here, I wish to bring forth some large patterns that emerge from writings on Kodagu. Continuing on the lines of Gover who saw specific moral values in minor languages and people who spoke them, these writings on Kodava construct the Kodavas as markedly different from the Hindu order and as definitely *not* belonging to the Brahminical order. Note that the term used by colonializers for Kodava is Coorg/Kurg and for Kannada it is Canarese.

I shall begin with a description from R. A. Cole's *Grammar of Coorg* which interestingly has many patterns combined.

This talook (Nalkanadu in Kodagu) is the very stronghold of Coorgs, and I found that many of them could not speak Canarese, the official language, but only a dialect, which I could not understand. The officials also when desirous of making remarks to each other, used to employ this dialect; and I was determined on trying to acquire it too. I was, however, much taken aback on learning that it was a mere patois (patua), and that Dr. Moegling, the celebrated German Missionary, to whom the cause of education in Coorg is so much indebted, had given up the attempt to learn the language, owing to the difficulty of conveying the exact pronunciation of the words. I have however, made an attempt by giving the Canarese letters for the written portion of this hitherto unknown dialect, and the Roman alphabet for the conveyance of the several peculiarities in pronunciation. ([ ... ] The attempt, poor as it as, has been preserved in and is offered to the philologist, better acquainted with the cognate languages of India, to decide as to what language and languages it has been derived from; and thereby ascertain, if possible, the origin of this peculiar/ and most interesting race of warlike mountaineers. (Cole 1867, 4)

Look at the contradictions in this one long paragraph. Kodava is marked as a dialect while simultaneously maintaining that it is a dialect that an outsider cannot comprehend at all. So, mutual intelligibility is not a criteria again to differentiate language and dialect. A dialect is based on who speaks it, and the power they wield. They are not speakers of the *official* Canarese. A dialect as something that is not official as opposed to Canarese, a dialect as something that is *patois*, *patua*, local parlance, *patua* as belonging to a particular region not belonging to the centre, something whose status is low. It is a dialect that is hitherto unknown, a discovery made possible by the British presence. What I would also want to note is the manner in which the British see themselves as preserving the language and offering it to the better acquainted to further explore, discover the origin of this peculiar but interesting race of warlike mountaineers. These people who speak Kodava/Coorg are not just different in their language but are also a different people from those of the plains. They are mountaineers, warlike and unpredictable in contrast to the usual colonial stereotype of effeminate caste/plains people.

One should also note how simultaneously there is an effort to establish an affinity to other languages of southern India and an effort to establish a difference as well, as in the manner of pronunciation which caused Moegling to abandon learning Kodava and made Cole find Kodava extremely difficult. The affinity and difference among languages both worked to serve as a source to chart the nature of race, to make sense of its difference, to connect to the races that were already mapped and known. Further from Cole:

> Coorgs were subjugated and their rajahs were Lingayats and foreigners; but as yet they have preserved their nationality intact. Their costumes, their manners and customs are peculiar and different from those of other races, occupying the adjoining countries. They strongly object to any interference on the part of Brahmins and their religion is as simple and pure as any heathen religion can be. (Cole 1867, 12)

The above is a reasoning as to how not all communities can be seen as part of the Brahminical structure, not part of a structure that is power–linear. Instances such as these, I argue, asserted the autonomy of communities as Kodavas, clearly marking the diverse nature of existence away from the caste. What this did is provide a new lens to view various communities and also provide a ground for these communities to imagine an identity that is independent, indigenous.

German missionary Rev. Moegling was one of the first missionaries in Coorg who took forward this notion of the unlettered but independent Coorgs a little further.

> The whole coorg-race was unlettered from the beginning their own priest-hood also, like the priests of ancient Germany and Britain, had no need of books ... The Coorgs have always been an unlettered people. To the present day, they are very ignorant and consequently very superstitious (26). These illiterate and untameable hunters seem to have ever had an instinctive antipathy to and thorough contempt for the sanctities and pretensions of the smooth and crafty brahman. Both Basava and the Brahmans, however, have been unable to make much of the mountain-race of Coorg. (Moegling 1855, 12)

In the very same book and even in Cole's there are multiple places where they constantly talk about the non-Hindu nature of the Coorgs, and how Brahmins with their books and *puranas* and superstitions were unable to bring the Coorgs into their fold. Being lettered, the Brahmins were unable to legitimize and control the Coorgs with whom the colonizers were able to establish a much better relationship. A cursory look at the census of the province of the Coorg from 1871 to 1931 also maps the number of Coorgs, as separate from the number of Hindus.[11]

In 1875, Lewis Rice, a historian and archaeologist who worked in the education department, wrote a huge body of texts on various aspects of South India, including Coorg. The three most prominent of the colonial administrators and missionaries, Moegling, Richter, and Rice follow a similar argument when it comes to the role of the Brahmin:

> Strictly speaking, no Brahman is a native of Coorg. Most of these who style themselves as such are descendants of families who settled in the country about a century ago. Left to the support of the Coorgs alone, they would long ago succumbed to starvation, for the essential Coorg customs and religious practices can have little in common with Brahminism. (Rice 1876, 204)

---

[11] Census records.

Whether the colonizer wanted to undermine the superiority of the Brahmin by using communities such as Coorgs and build alliances with different communities using their policy of 'divide and rule' is a question that can be raised. But given the authority of the Brahmin that was/is all pervasive among caste groups and given that these observations of the colonizer hold true to this day, one can safely argue that the colonizer's discourse and patronizing efforts in lettering and educating the Coorgs also brought in a new mobility which was almost impossible in the Brahmin–Lingayat caste complex—not just for Coorgs but for other minoritized communities as well.

## In Conclusion

We see that there are a whole lot of values assigned to languages that are oral, that lay in the realm of performative practices outside of caste. These writings do not cast these languages and the people who speak them in singular frames. Values are not laid in their skills of writing but in their practices that belonged to realms of orality. 'Writing is fixing, giving an idea a kind of material immortality ... an exalted fate that common speech does not deserve' (Kaviraj 2009, 315). Claims that argued for democracy (outside the caste fold), accessibility, moral authority, are contrasted with claims of superior civilizations and both these contradictions are present in discourses by Europeans and nationalists that placed language at the centre of colonial and nationalist politics.

With colonialism, combined with the already existing notions of knowledge associated with languages of gods, came in new linguistic habits, new 'cultural disposition for imagining the world and for securing one's place in that world' as Ramaswamy points out (254). This largely meant a very strategic revision of what was construed as ancient tradition and the authentic. In cases of languages such as Tamil, Kannada, Telugu, and Bangla this happened through what many have observed as imaginative combinations and complex interplay of 'new and old', 'west and orient', 'tradition and modernity'. While in these languages and many others, prose grew enormously in the late nineteenth and early twentieth centuries both by imagining and consolidating a past to be proud of, it also moulded itself into newer, modern forms such as the novel. While these binaries can be called into question from a range of positions, for 'small' languages, there was nothing 'old' despite their practices being 'primitive' and beyond the 'civilized' written cultures, oral was not ancient glory nor modern, one was never there nor here. That the colonizer propelled these 'old' oralities into the public realm, into the written realm in a way that was never witnessed before is a beginning of a new form.

# References

Ambedkar, B. R. 1955. *Thoughts on Linguistic States of India. Ambedkar, B. R. 'Thoughts on Linguistic States'.* http://ambedkar.org/ambcd/05A.%20Thoughts%20on%20Linguistic%20States%20Part%20I.htm

Ambedkar, B. R. (2002). 'Is There a Case for Pakistan?'. In *The Essential Writings of B. R. Ambedkar*, ed. Valerian Rodrigues, pp. 459–470. New Delhi: Oxford University Press.

Asad, Talal. 1986. 'The Concept of Cultural Translation in British Social Anthropology'. In *Writing Culture: The Poetics and Politics of Ethnography*, eds James Clifford and George E. Marcus, pp. 141–164. Berkeley and Los Angeles, CA: University of California Press.

Baumann, Richard and Charles Briggs. 2003. *Voices of Modernity: Language Ideologies and the Politics of Inequality*. Cambridge: Cambridge University Press.

Bourdieu, Pierre. 1991. *Language and Symbolic Power*. Introduction and ed. John B. Thompson, trans. Gino Raymond and Matthew Adamson. Cambridge: Polity Press.

Caldwell, Bishop Robert. 1875. *A Comparative Grammar of the Dravidian or South-Indian Languages*. London: Trubner and Co.

Chatterji, Suniti Kumar. 1971. '"Adivasi" Literatures of India: The Uncultivated "Adivasi" Languages'. *Indian Literature* 14 (3): 5–42.

Cole, R. A. 1867. *An Elementary Grammar of the Coorg Language*. Bangalore: Wesleyan Mission Press.

Cotton, Arthur. 1857. *A Study of Living Languages*. Madras: Scottish Press.

Emeneau, M. B. 1994a. 'The Languages of the Nilgiris'. In *Dravidian Studies: Selected Papers*, ed. Bh. Krishnamurthy, pp. 387–398. Delhi: Motilal Banarsidas Publishers.

Emeneau, M. B. 1994b. 'Linguistic Archaisms in Toda Songs'. In *Dravidian Studies: Selected Papers* ed. Bh. Krishnamurthy, pp. 287–302. Delhi: Motilal Banarsidas Publishers.

Gandhi, M. K. 1947. *Rashtrabhasha Hindustani*. Ahmedabad: Navjivan.

Ghosh, Anindita. 2006. *Power in Print: Popular Publishing and Politics of Language and Culture in a Colonial Society*. New Delhi: Oxford University Press.

Gover, E. Charles. 1871. *The Folk-songs of Southern India*. London: Higginbotham and Company.

Graeter, A. 1870. *Coorg Songs*. Mangalore: Basel Mission Press.

Grierson, G. A. 1906. *Linguistic Survey of India: Vol. 4, Munda and Dravidian Languages*. Calcutta: Office of the Superintendent of Government Printing, India.

Grierson, G. A. 1927. *Linguistic Survey of India:* Vol. 1, Part 1, *Introductory.* Calcutta: Government of India Central Publication Branch.

Joseph, Tony. 2018. *Early Indians: The Story of Our Ancestors and Where We Came From.* New Delhi: Juggernaut.

Jotirao Phule. 2008. *Slavery.* New Delhi: Critical Quest.

Kar, Bodhisattva. 2008. '"Tongue Has No Bone"; Fixing the Assamese Language, *c.* 1800–*c.* 1930'. *Studies in History* 24 (1): 27–76.

Kaviraj, Sudipta. 2009. 'Writing, Speaking, Being: Language and the Historical Formation of Identities in India'. In *Language and Politics in India*, ed. Asha Sarangi, pp. 312–350. New Delhi: Oxford University Press.

Kaviraj, Sudipta. 2010. *The Imaginary Institution of India: Politics and Ideas.* New York: Columbia University Press.

Kothari, Rita. 2017b. 'Grierson's Linguistic Survey of India: Acts of Naming and Translating'. In *The Multilingual Nation: Translation and Language Dynamics in India*, ed. Rita Kothari, pp. 116–132. New Delhi: Oxford University Press.

Mallikarjun, B. 1993. *A Descriptive Analysis of Yerava.* Mysore: Central Institute of Indian Languages.

Manoharan, Karthik R. 2021. 'Radical freedom: Periyar and women'. (https://doi.org/10.12688/openreseurope.13131.1). 1:6

Mitchell, Lisa. 2009. *Language, Emotion, and Politics in South India: The Making of a Mother Tongue.* Ranikhet: Permanent Black.

Moegling, Herman. 1855. *Coorg Memoirs: An Account of Coorg Memoirs and of the Coorg Mission.* Bangalore: Wesleyan Missionary Press.

Mohan, Peggy. 2021. *Wanderers, Kings, Merchants. The Story of India Through Its Languages.* Gurugram: Penguin Viking.

Nagaraj, D. R. 2012. *Listening to the Loom. Essays on Literature, Politics and Violence*, ed. Prithvi Datta Chandra Shobhi. New Delhi: Permanent Black.

Nair, Janaki. 1996. '"Memories of Underdevelopment": Language and Its Identities in Contemporary Karnataka'. *Economic and Political Weekly* 31 (41–42): 2809–2816.

Nair, Janaki. 2011. *Mysore Modern. Rethinking the Region Under Princely Rule.* Hyderabad: Orient Blackswan.

Naregal, Veena. 2001. *Language Politics, Elites, and the Public Sphere: Western India Under Colonialism.* Ranikhet: Permanent Black.

Niveditha, K. 2018. 'Print, Colonialism and the Early Malayalee Public Sphere: Discourses of Language Reform and Linguistic Nationalism (1820–1920)'. Unpublished PhD Dissertation submitted to the University of Hyderabad. Hyderabad.

Prasad, Madhava. 2014. 'The Political Commons: Language and the Nation State Form'. *Critical Quarterly* 56 (3): 92–105.

Rahman, Tariq. 2019. *Book Reviews* http://www.bloomsburypakistan.org/.Majeed,Javed.

Ramaswamy, Sumathy. 1997. *Passions of the Tongue: Language Devotion in Tamil India, 1891–1970.* Berkeley, CA: University of California Press.

Rao, Surendra and K. M. Lokesh. 1998. *Coorg Invented: Nineteenth-Century European Writings on Kodagu.* Madikeri: Forum for Kodagu Studies.

Reddy, Manohar N. 2015. 'Modernity of Telugu: Language Politics and National Identity'. Unpublished PhD Dissertation submitted to the English and Foreign Languages University. Hyderabad.

Rice, Lewis. 1876. *Mysore and Coorg: A Gazetteer*. Bangalore: Mysore Government Press.

Richter, G. 1870. *Gazetteer of Coorg*. New Delhi: Low Price Publications.

Somayyaji, Pattabhirama. 2002. 'Chartering Carceral Society: Kodagu-Linguistically Speaking'. In *Linguistic Landscaping in India with Particular Reference to the New States*, eds N. H. Itagi and Shailendra Kumar Singh, pp. 139–153. Mysore: Central Institute of Indian Languages.

Tharakeshwar, V. B. 2003. 'Translating Nationalism: The Politics of Language and Community'. *Journal of Karnataka Studies* 1 (1): 5–59.

Thurston, Edgar. 1913. *Provincial Geographies of India*. Vol. 3, *The Madras Presidency with Mysore, Coorg and the Associated States*. Cambridge: Cambridge University Press.

Upadhyaya, Himanshu. 2010. 'Gandhi, Gujarati Spelling and the Ideology of Standardisation'. *Economic and Political Weekly* 45 (24): 26–33.

# 2

# Three Writers, Three Languages, and the Contradictions of a Kodava Identity

The idea of translation as representation or indeed representation as translation is now an established one. Since the times of postcolonial theory, especially from Edward Said (1978), Tejaswini Niranjana (1992), and Talal Asad (1986), translation and representation have been inseparable. In her seminal work *Siting Translation: History, Post-Structuralism, and the Colonial Context*, Tejaswini Niranjana has shown how translation has long been a site for perpetuating the unequal relations among peoples, races, and languages. How has translation helped the colonializer to construct 'others' as exotic and outside history is the question she explores. Translation became a project that aided and cemented colonial power via texts that translated a whole people belonging to the entire subcontinent and elsewhere as well. This is a point that is further elaborated by Talal Asad in his 'The Concept of Cultural Translation in British Social Anthropology' (1986). The social authority of the anthropologist (aided by the powers of colonialism and other institutions of power) tends to reduce and simplify 'the implicit meanings of subordinate societies', for, the process of cultural translation is inescapably caught up in relations of power (Asad, 163).

What is important for this chapter is the manner in which Niranjana, Asad, and others use translation as representation to underscore the structural inequalities between groups in society. Bringing translation as representation into our picture inevitably brings in the language question and this allows us to see how languages and peoples who speak them are part of these strategies that represent them. It also allows us to see the strategies of translation that are used by the represented to engage, negotiate, resist in a manner that ruptures the narrative, complicates the identities of not only the represented but that of the representer as well.

*Languages of Minority.* Sowmya Dechamma CC, Oxford University Press. © Oxford University Press 2024.
DOI: 10.1093/oso/9780198908456.003.0003

Where this chapter deviates from Niranjana and Asad is in its reconsideration of relationships between the colonized and the colonizer. I do this based on the translations and representations of Kodava people of themselves as narrated by themselves. It also sees translation as forging a new identity via such representations. Although the three texts I analyse vary in their strategy, vary in their ideology, and vary in their translation of Kodava identity, this translation implied a very different relationship with the colonizer, different from the anti-colonial stance. In effect, almost all three texts see writing as an act that translated the Kodava from an unlettered realm to a lettered one. This scripting of Kodava is made possible only by the education brought in by the English in the latter half of the nineteenth century. Not just that these texts show a different relationship with the colonizer, but they also translate the Kodava as different, autonomous, and therefore build a relationship of difference, if not oppositional with the dominant Hindu. This is where I intend to extend and question postcolonial ideas of translation. Translation of identities, especially for minority communities, had an immense bearing in the claiming of themselves as separate from the Brahminical structure, and often as victims of that caste structure. The act of formal education, the act of writing, the act of translating—all enabled by the colonizer—provided the much-needed platform for the emergence of a refashioned distinct self and of a possibility of resistance to dominant modes of representation. How the first three available texts by Kodavas do this is the focus of this chapter. If translation theories have largely focused on how translation consolidated and negotiated powers between colonizer and colonized, this chapter seeks to understand how translation destabilized long-existing power relationships among the colonized, among the hierarchized communities of India, and the unwitting role the colonizers and their policies played in this destabilization. I want to emphasize that the Kodava relationship with the colonizer leaves us with many more questions, questions that hint at the tensions between Brahminism and colonialism, hint at alliances between backward class/Dalit/Adivasi communities and the colonizer since the times of Jotiba Phule. The argument here is how translation aided by the colonizer helped the Kodava people and language, ushering in new ideas, new ways of life, and translating Kodavas into a new realm. This, needless to say, includes introducing writing, ushering in translation, and articulation in public for Kodavas and non-Kodavas alike.

While trying to examine the nature of early writings in Kodava/ Kannada/English by Kodavas that used the Kannada script, the chapter seeks to answer how writing in a language of the minority can be understood as translation in itself. How did they foreground and translate a different identity for and of the Kodava, different from that of the majority Kannada-speaking Hindu-caste self? These questions, the chapter argues, are significant in the present context when attempts are on to write Kodava and other linguistic minorities into the dominant narratives of Hinduism. I try to answer these questions by analysing three early texts in and on Kodava written by three Kodava men. The texts in question are Koravanda Appaiah's *Kodavara Kulaachaaradi Tatvojeevini* (*An Explication of Kodava Life and Customs*, 1902), a text that is almost forgotten despite being written twenty-two years ahead of *Pattole Palame* (*Words on Silk*, 1924) by Nadikerianda Chinnappa, a text that is known and is popular with the Kodava public. The third text is Appaneravanda Appacha's (popularly known as Haradasa Appacha Kavi) *Naal Naataka* (*Four Plays*, written between 1906 and 1918). I do not just see the texts in question as being translated and translatable, but also contexts and everyday practices as being translated and translatable at all times. This act of translating, of putting in writing what was spoken, what was sung, and what was narrated orally was seen as worthy as writing in the original. Needless to say, this act of scripting, which I see as translating the spoken to the written word, was facilitated by the colonial British. The long Lingayat[1] rule of Kodagu from around 1600 until 1834 when the British took over, did not see any writing and translations of Kodava, either by Kodavas or non-Kodavas. During this period, albeit the Lingayat origin being anti-Brahmin, the practices of writing and of translation were restricted to the court, and restricted to the castes and classes that required chronicling. Despite the tenuous relationship Kodavas had with the Lingayat kings, Kodavas neither found the need nor perhaps found the context to write, to document, to translate, or to record by the means of script. This comes close to what James Scott (2009) has succinctly termed as 'advantages of orality' that a community practised to keep the all-too-powerful state at an arms' length. Oral history can be strategic, it can be

---

[1] Kodagu was ruled by Kannada-speaking Kings, followers of Lingayat or Veerashaiva religion, outsiders to the region of Kodagu.

used when and how the community needs it. It could be transformed, translated as and when required. There are no permanent enemies or friends in a history that is oral. The history in its oral form belonged to everyone who wanted to know it, to hear it, and required no prerequisite training of the eye, of the script to decipher it, to use it. It is everyone's history that could be sung, told, danced to, and to be part of. Once translated to script, history ceases to be democratic, ceases to be strategic. But then, why did the Kodavas take to translating and writing with the advent of the British? This is something that we cannot explain using Scott's theory and needs further examination.

*Kodavara Kulaachaaradi Tatvojeevini* written in Kannada is a description of Kodava customs with an in-text critical analysis by the author; *Pattole Palame* is a book in three languages, an innovation of sorts—in Kodava, Kannada, and some English—is a compilation of Kodava customs, songs, sayings, rituals, and community-based literature; and *Naal Naataka* in Kodava is as the name suggests, a compilation of the four plays of the author. They are very different in their purpose, in their use of language, and in the contexts in which they were written and circulated. What is central to my chapter is not the customs, rituals, songs, or the plays that constitute these texts but the manner in which the texts translated the Kodava identity via the scripted word. This can be better understood by analysing the texts' prefaces, forewords, afterwords, and epilogues written by the authors, translators, and publishers. Therefore, despite the genres of these texts being vastly different, they hold crucial insights to the construction of an ethnolinguistic minority and their translated entry into a scripted realm.

## *Pattole Palame*: Orality and Translation

When Nadikerianda Chinnappa published his magnum opus *Pattole Palame* in 1924, he was a police officer in the British-ruled Coorg. His relationship, and in fact, the relationship of most Kodavas to English, both the language and the people, has mostly been expressed in terms that are grateful if not reverent. All his benefactors felt it was good to publish the literature of Kodava in print form in order to prevent 'customs from being forgotten, from being wrongly practised by mistake, and since it would bring in uniformity among changing practices' (Chinnappa 1924, i–ii). This is along the lines of seeing changing practices as translation of practices, of seeing many translations of a practice which is then standardized via written translation.

The title page of *Pattole Palame* reads: '*Kodavada Pattole Palame:* Nadikerianda Chinnappa (*Ivarinda Sangrahisalpattaddu* [compiled by this person])'. Although Chinnappa did compile the lore and customs of Kodavas, the book also consists of considerable explanation by him of what he compiled. It also has a brief history of Coorg/Kodagu and also included the national anthem of Kodagu, which was Chinnappa's own composition. But what interested me is that despite the copyright of the book being registered, Chinnappa remains the compiler, not the author. Compiling the literature of his community and translating it into the scripted word does not give him the authority of authorship. The lore is the community's, not his alone. He is only the translator–compiler. This, as A. K. Ramanujan (1991) has shown us, deviates from the long history of claiming authorship of Hindu epics (*Ramayana* and *Mahabharata*) rewritten throughout medieval history in many Indian languages until around the twentieth century. In what Sujit Mukherjee (1994) has called 'translation as new writing', the written history in Indian languages for centuries saw translations as new writing and assigned the name of the translator/recreator as the author of the recreated work. Although they were totally transformed versions of the fluid epics, one cannot but see how oral cultures even in the twentieth century did not attempt to claim absolute authority over a text even when the author had an inkling that it was a harbinger of change.

Why did Chinnappa start on this mission of compilation of literature thus far oral in nature? 'It seemed to me that the customs were like "*aar naadk noor paaje*": a hundred tongues for six villages'.[2] Following this, Chinnappa says he realized some customs were forgotten, some were just left out, some moved here and there with some additions and deletions. Despite the difference being inconsequential, they demanded a reform into an '*ekibhaava*, a uniform expression' and Chinnappa found it compelling enough to put orality in the script form and began writing (Chinnappa 1924, i).

---

[2] All translations are mine unless otherwise specified.

This kind of translation that aims at a corrective, that aims at a uniformed expression, that attempts at making orality's (and translation's) fluidity into something rigid, is not new. What is significant is that he saw the Kodava identity as being constituted by songs, words, and practices—an identity that he recognized as changing. He did not attempt to construct an identity and locate it within the glory of written literature, he did not mourn the lack of written literature. For him, an identity based on orality was good with a little bit of reform towards uniformity.

I want to spend a little time on noting the relationship between writing down customs as against practising them. According to Chinnappa, writing down: will, firstly, not let us forget, will let us remember in one more way, adding to the innumerable ways of remembering orality through practice. And secondly, it will enable us not to mistakenly forget or wrongly practise our customs/rituals—thus leaving little chance for the vagaries of memory and the consequent shifting of practices (this is contingent on people not just reading *Pattole Palame* but also believing Chinnappa's version to be the 'correct' practice to be followed).[3] And thirdly, Chinnappa uses the term *ekibhaava*, a very Sanskritized Kannada term that is not used even in spoken Kannada, let alone in Kodava. *Ekibhaava*, as mentioned means 'uniform expression', and to Chinnappa's mind, this uniformity could be brought about only via writing (Chinnappa, i–ii). There is a very clear and conscious manner in which writing is seen in contradiction to orality and its varied practices. This is a claim for 'authenticity' in translation, and it is interesting to note that shifting and changing practices do not seem natural to Chinnappa. Practices could not exist in the realm of translation, forever shifting. They had to be uniformized and the means by which this could possibly be achieved is by scripting the oral, an act of translation in itself, self-translation to be more precise (Chinnappa, i–ii).

Chinnappa's anxiety towards an authentic, uniform practice also suggests the coming of the new world of script and print. In fact, the varying

---

[3] Many people from the south of Kodagu, a region known as *Kiggat naad*, mentioned how Nadikerianda Chinnappa's compilation was limited to *Mendale naad*, a region close to the centre of power throughout known Kodagu history, be it Lingayat kings or the British. From the language spoken, customs and performative practices, to socio-economic conditions, *Kiggat naad* varies drastically from *Mendale naad*. *Kiggat* has also been perceived and represented as 'undesirable', 'uncouth', and 'uncultured' in relation to *Mendale*.

nature of performative practices become visible and become undesirable only in this new world of script and print. Uniformity becomes desirable when writing became available. But then, this is a writing that is in the service of practices, not in the service of an identity built on written history, but towards an identity of practices, even if it desired uniformity.

There also exist contradictions and variations while compiling texts. Compiling a chosen variety, using a certain word, certain phrase, certain verse, certain meaning over others available is a process that can be understood only as translation, a process that *is* translation. I also want to emphasize that for Chinnappa, writing is not an exalted, sacred form over and above other forms. It is only a means, a process through which Kodava customs and practices could be strengthened, perhaps refined. There is hardly a binary between written and oral, between the unlettered and lettered, between scripted and the spoken word, between print and the performative, unlike the ones created by most colonial and non-Kodava ethnographers. Oral is not primitive, it is *us*. The 'lack of script' is not an issue at all. Perhaps it was an advantage and therefore Chinnappa could use Kannada, Kodava, and English—the three languages used in his book.

One of the most significant things Chinnappa does is to write 'The Coorg National Anthem'. This is a poem/song in praise of Kodagu. The poem's title is in English, and the subtitle in very Sanskritized Kannada is '*Swadesha Priya Keerthane*' ('An Ode to One's Beloved Country', Chinnappa, iii). Interestingly, the song is in Kodava. The anthem praises and offers prayers to the River Kaaveri, the holy river of the people of Kodagu.

> *Sri Mula Kanniye*[4]
> O mother Kaveri,
> Wear *pommale*[5] Kodagu as a garland, O Mother!
> Why do you need a *jommaale?*[6]
> Why do you need a garland of flowers?
> Wear the golden land of Kodagu as a garland, O mother!

---

[4] 'O primeval sacred maiden'. The translation of the song is by Bovverianda Nanjamma and Chinnappa (2003), their translation retains the first line in Kodava.

[5] Roughly meaning a gold chain.

[6] Traditional Kodava jewellery worn by women. A chain of two strands of gold beads, threaded on black or gold strings (Nanjamma and Chinnappa, 5).

The song has two more paragraphs exalting Kaaveri. Although the stanza quoted above reads very simple, we need to look at it from the lens of 'The Coorg National Anthem', the title given to the song by Chinnappa. Kodagu is a world in itself. For a nature-goddess like Kaaveri (despite Hindu mythologies associated with her), Kodagu's exemplary qualities are more than enough. Kaaveri is the mother and Kodagu is the world/nation that can make Kaaveri shine. Why does a Kodava *desha*, the Kodava nation, need a national anthem? Remember, Chinnappa is writing this in 1922, just around the time a national anthem was conceptualized for the Indian nation. For ages, until now, Kodagu has been referred to by its people as Kodagu *naad* or Kodagu *desha*, the Kodagu Land or Kodagu nation, despite their contested loyalties to the ruling state—be it monarchic, colonial, or democratic, the notion that their land is a nation in itself and it needed a distinct anthem suggests an identity that is not easy to contain within the idea of a powerful majoritarian state. Not just easy to contain but also not easy to translate into the practices of the majoritarian state and its community. Chinnappa clearly was conscious of a Kodava identity that demanded different translations, distinct from the ones that were etched in the glories of written, documented history, literary or history proper.

Chinnappa's book, a compilation of customs, rituals, performative practices, and songs during major events of Kodava life, death, and festivals, also has a smattering of documented history of the rule of the Lingayat kings, and a geographical and climatic description of Kodagu. Chinnappa saw all this as part of indigenous practices and did not ever in his explanations and explications try to bring in a Hindu logic to Kodava identity. Indeed, he wrote of Kodava as an autonomous community, outside the Hindu religious and caste fold. This as we can see is translating the Kodava identity as different, as not so legible to the Hindu and/or colonial state, unlike what Koravanda Appaiah wrote in 1902.

### *Kodavara Kulaachaaradi Tatvojeevini:* Trans-creation of a 'Different' Hindu Self

*Kodavara Kulaachaaradi Tatvojeevini* ('An Explication of Kodava Life and Customs'), is a text from 1902 that was almost unknown until it was translated into Kodava from Kannada in 2003. The translation published by the government's Karnataka Kodava Sahitya Akademi (Karnataka Kodava Literary Organization) in 2003, gave the text some visibility, although *Pattole Palame* and *Naal Naataka* hold the popular imagination of Kodava and non-Kodavas alike as the first and most important written texts on Kodava literature, culture, and history by Kodavas. Nadikerianda Chinnappa has mentioned in one of his texts as to how Appaiah, *Kodavara Kulaachaaradi Tatvojeevini*'s author, had translated the *Bhagavat Gita* into Kodava. Although all three writers analysed here were contemporaries, except for Chinnappa's mention of Appaiah, there is no mention of each other in any of their texts that are available today.

*Kodavara Kulaachaaradi Tatvojeevini* was written in Kannada by Dr Koravanda Appaiah, the first medical doctor from the Kodava community. He served the Mysore princely state in various capacities, and was the palace surgeon for the Mysore king. Appaiah was also a member of the Theosophical Society in Chennai and we will see how this possibly influenced his thoughts and writing. He was a polyglot who knew Kodava, Tamil, Malayalam, Telugu, Tulu, English, and Hindustani. His first text is known to have been published in 1884 and he is also credited with devising a new, separate script for Kodava. Unfortunately, neither of these is available today. In effect, Appaiah was literally the foremost in scripting the language and culture of Kodava. In his preface Appaiah mentions how the death of his only child pushed him to do something good for the community and this is the reason behind the writing of the book (Appaiah 1902, 7). *Kodavara Kulaachaaradi Tatvojeevini* is a small book. The translator of this book from Kannada to Kodava, Theethira Rekha Vasanth mentions that the copy she acquired had some pages missing from the end of the book. The full book is not known to be available anywhere. I have read only the Kodava translation of 2003 since the Kannada original is not available.

Both the translator and the publisher make a point of emphasizing that Dr Koravanda Appaiah was the first 'native scholar' (ii–iv) from Kodagu who wrote on Kodagu and Kodavas. Although being a 'native scholar' is recognized, they do not address the question of why Appaiah writes the book in Kannada, a non-native language for him. This question of native is important since, until Appaiah the only material on Kodagu and

Kodavas was by Europeans of various hues.[7] But then, as I mentioned at the beginning of this chapter, the colonial enterprise worked in favour of many minority communities,—Dalit, backward castes, Adivasis and indigenous ethnolinguistic minorities like Kodavas. This is not to say that the privileged castes did not benefit from colonial enterprises, be it education or otherwise. They benefited hugely. But the fact that it served different purposes to different communities and shaped the politics and histories to come is yet to be strongly articulated.

My analysis of *Kodavara Kulaachaaradi Tatvojeevini* is based on the Kodava translation. This comes close to the idea that Mini Chandran (2017) charts in her essay 'Dancing in the Hall of Mirrors' where she talks about how there can never be one reading of a text, especially of a translated text. Translations are like reflections in a hall of mirrors, dancing, performing all the time. My reading of the translation alone, and not of the 'original' contributes to these performative meanings, specifically because of the orality of Kodava. Appaiah writing about Kodavas in Kannada in 1902, Rekha Vasanth translating it into Kodava in 2003, me writing about all of this in English in 2019, suggests various levels of meanings generated via various processes of translation across a century. The translator Theethira Rekha Vasanth in her acknowledgement discusses how challenging the process of translation was. 'There has been a century's difference added to the challenge of not finding an appropriate equivalence in Kodava for some Kannada words which Koravanda Appaiah used. This has made me retain the Kannada words. There is no other way for a language to move forward other than this (Vasanth 2003, xv)'. Lucia Boldrini's (2010) understanding of how languages work in relation to cultural and political legitimacy is telling in this discussion of Kannada and Kodava. 'Adopting the topos of *translatio studii et imperii* ("translation of culture and knowledge, and of political power and legitimacy") requires that the claimants prove that they are worthy of their newly acquired power. This is achieved, among other things, through the activity of imitation and translation' (Boldrini, 194), which Boldrini suggests are transformative activities. This open acknowledgement of Rekha Vasanth of Kannada being better and richer points to how it is only when

---

[7] Among many administrators and missionaries who wrote on Kodagu/Coorg, Moegling (1855), Richter (1870), Rice (1878), are well known.

a language is written, in effect translated, does its 'deficiencies' become visible. The problem of untranslatability is an issue with 'lesser' languages. We need to also remember that never does the spoken word encounter this problem of deficiency or lack which has been a constant companion of translation since the times of biblical translation. It is only when words are scripted that the problem of untranslatability crops up, untranslatable from the legitimate language to the not so legitimate one. In this world of writing, it is the larger and smaller imperialisms, colonizations that have the wherewithal to represent, to translate, to document.

Appaiah begins his text with a direct attack on Europeans and their mechanisms of representations, and their use of language:

> Some Europeans like Connor, Moegling, Richter, Rice have written a few things about Kodavas. But none of them knew the Kodava language ... Connor mentions that during the time he was writing, the King had ordered people not to speak the truth to any white man. [ ... ] in such a situation, very less of what these Europeans wrote seem to be correct. (Appaiah, 1)

What is then the relationship between ethnography, documentation, and language, be it colonial or contemporary ones? Can one write or translate into another language what they cannot understand? What languages did the Europeans use to 'gather' their information—English, Kannada? Not Kodava unless it was through a translator who knew both Kodava and English. How many translation performances in the hall of mirrors then would such a process take in order to establish a certain truth of meaning?

Appaiah's argument is to largely debunk select colonial theories and contextualize the Kodava as not very different from the Hinduism of the Mysore palace where he largely lived and also in the context of the Theosophical society of which he was part. Appaiah provides his logic as to why Kodavas do not belong to the Kadamba dynasty's lineage as noted by Lewis Rice (1878); he also argues how the *Kaaveri Purana* (story of the River Kaaveri which has its origin in the hills of Kodagu) is irrational since it talks about Kodavas being the offspring of a Kshyatriya king and a Shudra woman who bore a hundred sons. 'What could be the life-time of a woman who bore a hundred children, that too all men?'

(Appaiah, 3) The mention of '*mleccha*' in *Kaaveri purana* is also a point of contention. Appaiah points out that only Muslims are referred to as *mlecchas*[8] and since Muslims have been in India for not more than five hundred years, can the River Kaaveri be only five hundred years old? The facts of the matter apart, what is interesting for me is that Appaiah is debunking much of Brahminical literature related to the story of Kaaveri, but is ascribing the Brahminical literature to Europeans! But then, he uses another European, Holland's 'history' to prove how Kodavas were descendants of Chalukyas, the powerful dynasty that ruled much of the south and parts of central India between the sixth and twelfth centuries (Appaiah, 4). Whether Holland knew Kodava, how much of Kodava history did he know, how much time had he spent in the region, and whether the king's order of not speaking the truth to foreigners played a role in Holland's scheme: questions asked regarding other Europeans' work are not asked. Appaiah also uses *Manusmriti*, quotes from it occasionally to substantiate Holland's point and at times to justify certain Kodava practices. Some of Holland's observations Appaiah subscribes to are racist, to say the least. He names the Kodavas as belonging to 'good races' (the Kodava terms used are *nalla jaati* and *nalla kula,* meaning 'good caste' and 'good clan/caste group') (Appaiah, 18) since their appearance differs from the people around them. Appaiah uses this to show Kodavas are of Kshatriya stock from the north of the Vindhya mountains (what happens to the Chalukyas, who were definitely from the south and whose descendants according to him are Kodavas remains a puzzle (Appaiah, 18–19). Beginning with the late nineteenth century, many communities, especially the non-Hindu ones and the ones lowered in the caste structure, began claiming a status in the caste order by constructing histories and a past where their origins are said to be 'warrior caste' or Kshatriyas. Appaiah does the same.

He also talks about why Kodavas do not wear the thread across their shoulders like many Kshatriyas do (4)? Why do Kodava women wear the head scarf only ceremonially (5)? How the Kodava men's initiation into hunting and agriculture can be seen as *upanayana*, a twice-born ritual of Brahmin and Kshyatriyas? The justification for all these come from

---

[8] *Mleccha* can mean several things in Sanskrit literature, ranging from 'foreigner', 'barbaric', 'uncouth'.

*Manusmriti* and at times from *Ramayana*. Some very crucial concerns as to why there has never been (or never is even today) a Brahmin in all Kodava rituals of life and death, why Kodava festivals are not around any Hindu god, why pork and alcohol are central to every celebration and mourning, how ancestral worship is central to all Kodava practices, how remarriage and widow remarriage are customary, how child marriage does not exist, how women and men light the pyre of the deceased none of these warrant an elaboration in his work. Some of his translations of Kodava words and practices are outrightly way off the mark. His translation of a Kodava practice called *okka parije* (Appaiah, 43), a practice where a man moves to the wife's clan/house is this: '*okka* is a derivation of *Uga*, meaning someone who has left his belonging, *parije* means the Sanskrit *praja*, or people'. *Okka* is the endogamous clan among Kodavas and to this day, '*okka*' is a term, concept, and category practised very consciously. *Okka parije* is a practice of marriage where the man marries into the clan of the woman when there is no male heir on the woman's side. Appaiah's elaboration is geared towards showing how a male child is born, grows, and dies following the four stages of life (*varnashrama*) of the upper-caste Hindu. Given that Appaiah is particular about logic in certain other aspects, how logical or rational *Manusmriti* is (that Kshatriyas are born from the god Brahma's shoulders) is a question Appaiah does not ask and also raises the question of its authorship. In fact, many of the European texts Appaiah dismisses mention how *Kaaveri Purana* is a cock-and-bull story.

Appaiah's rational self, perhaps an influence from his association with Theosophical Society makes him question the *puranas* and the apparent illogical nature of it. The attribution of 'lie' to the European and not to the Brahmin who created the literature that the European translated is in itself a translation of certain narratives. This translation of the Kodava from a Kshatriya past to the present and into the future also assumes importance for Appaiah since he claims the Pandyas who ruled Kodagu before the Chalukyas did not allow people to read and write, they were forced to forget their language, and had to learn Tamil. This for Appaiah was the reason why Kodavas could not write their own history. (Why did Kodavas not learn to read and write during Chalukyas and after Chalukyas(between the sixth century AD until the British came) is a question unanswered).

Rekha Vasanth commenting on how Appaiah located Kodava within the *Manusmriti* while Chinnappa did so within an indigenous Adivasi realm, notes that both texts situate Kodavas in completely contradictory spheres. The language they used is also different. Appaiah uses the old version of Kannada (*Hala Kannada)* and Chinnappa uses the newer form of Kannada (*Hosa Kannada)* in his multilingual text (x–xi). *Pattole Palame* stands as an autonomous text, without much critical referencing from outside, claiming an indigenous autonomous identity for Kodavas. Appaiah, on the other hand, brings in critical ideas of his own and of others to disprove certain colonial claims but uses another colonial text to validate the Kodava connection to Hinduism. Chinnappa worked for the colonial British and sought to translate the Kodava identity as an autonomous one, away from the colonizer's influence and away from the Brahminical narrative. Appaiah worked for the Mysore king, a Hindu, reformist, welfarist, whose rule Janaki Nair (2012) has termed 'Monarchical Modern'. Appaiah, surrounded by Brahmin *diwans* (ministers) and other privileged figures at court, might have felt the need to Hinduize unlike Chinnappa who saw an indigenous community in the Kodava while acknowledging his colonial benefactors who helped him publish his compilation. The Theosophist/doctor/king's surgeon meant reformed Hinduism, as against the colonizer but not against the benefactor's religion. These kinds of translations of the community, we then see happening within certain contexts that have shaped not just the authors but the community in question as well.

## *Sree Kaaveri Naataka:* Translation, Caste, and the Kodava

Born in 1868, Appaneravanda Appacha, popularly known as Haradasa Appacha Kavi, was the first ever among the Kodavas and others to write in a fictional genre, plays, in the Kodava language. This has bestowed on him the title of Aadikavi of Kodava, the first poet of Kodavas. Between 1906 and 1918 he wrote four plays: *Yayaati Raaja Naataka* (1906); *Savitri* (1908); *Subramanya* (1908); and *Sree Kaaveri Naataka* (1918). That these are stories from the Hindu *Puranas* (Hindu mythologies) and are in effect a new writing, new translation, new recreations, effectively following the practice of 'translation as new writing', which as mentioned has been a practice in major Indian languages until the arrival of print aided by capital. These recreations of *Ramayana* and *Mahabharata* were/are known as original writings, ascribed to the poet who wrote them and have been harbingers of innovations, small revolutions, not to mention newer traditions of writing. But as I shall argue, Appacha not just recreated the Sanskrit via Kannada translations, but questioned Sanskrit practices thereby transcending traditions as he translated.

Appacha's writing, though recognized, read, and staged as performances, did not set the tradition of Kodava writing anywhere in his lifetime. Appacha is also revered since he travelled from village to village in Kodagu, putting on performances of his plays. The edition of his plays I read was published as part of his centenary celebrations in 1968–1970. He worked for the Department of *Muzrai*, a government department that looks after Hindu temple affairs, a practice that has been in vogue since the colonial times (and before). This, like Dr Koravanda Appaiah, made Appacha study Hinduism and its stories and compelled him to translate and recreate some for his own people. He died very poor, blind, and unable to hear, after retiring early from the civil service.

'*Naataka, Saahitya, Kalek enn-na uur idalla*' ('This is not a place known for its plays, literature, and arts') is how B. D. Ganapathy, a noted Kodava writer in English and Kannada, begins his introduction of Appacha in the said volume (vi). I translate this as an idea that largely represents Kodagu to the world of written-language cultures. Largely seen as a lack, understanding literature and arts in the literal written sense, the performative practices and culture of Kodavas are thought to be 'different' if not of a second order. But I also see the possibility of Ganapathy saying 'this place has other, different possibilities, cultures, and that we are taking up writing now'. Writing and translating is an empowering act, especially when in interaction with more powerful cultures than one's own. Little wonder writing was barred for most communities, castes, and classes by the people in power. Remember Appaiah's logic of how reading and writing were denied by the rulers to Kodavas. Therefore, instead of interpreting Ganapthy's words in the negative, I see it as Appacha enabling the act of translating the written word for the Kodava, to make it accessible, and make it possible to question what is written.

In Appacha's words:

Honorable people, who is Shree Kaaveramme? How did she take birth, what are the reasons for her birth, why did she take the avatar of River Kaaveri? How did this country become the country of our birth? [ ... ] I doubt if my fellow country folk are aware of all these. I doubt this since the old Kaaveri Purana is in Sanskrit and all of us know that Sanskrit knowledge in this Kodagu country is non-existent. [ ... ] to avoid all difficulties with Sanskrit, I have sourced this story from many puranas, written it in Kodava language using Kannada letters so that every one of us can read and understand. I have taken this task so that generations to come will be aware of the Kodavas, that every Kodava will have this book at home, will remember and sing in praise of Kaaveri with devotion that will bring salvation to all. (Kavi 1918/2010, 1)

Appacha answers these questions within the play *Sree Kaaveri Purana*. But then, why is he translating from Sanskrit via Kannada? We need to remember that he worked with the department responsible for Hindu temples. He believes Sanskrit cannot be and will not be a medium through which everyone can attain salvation. It has to be through the vernacular. And it cannot be Kannada. It had to use the Kannada letters to translate the Sanskrit stories to Kodava. It is indeed a moment of vernacularization where the less powerful recreates the language and literature of the powerful even as it is consciously questioned. 'Sanskrit education is zero' are his exact words. Novetzke's work on vernacularization and its relation to religion in Marathi as discussed in the introduction, shows us that:

[A]t the confluence of literary vernacularization and the application of a religious ethics of salvation, a discursive sphere opens up in which questions of social inequality, particularly around caste and gender, rise to the surface of public debate. (Novetzke 2018, 150)

Perhaps Appacha knew the best way to address the privilege of Sanskrit is to translate it to Kodava, a language of orality, a language and people for whom Sanskrit meant very little. His attempt is to elevate Kodava into the realm of writing, vernacularizing it not just in terms of language but by infusing Kodava practices into what he writes. Not just this, there is a direct attack on how Brahmins kept learning the letters, Sanskrit or otherwise, to themselves, thereby excluding Kodavas and all others. This is best illustrated by some examples.

His plays constitute hundreds of songs, some devotional but many popular even to this day for their rhythm, fun, description of life, nature, and practices in Kodagu.

> *Nipp-l alepava bollavva*
> *Bolle kallavva*
> *Bolthith ullavva, chaayi-l ullavva*
> *Chaayi-l ullavva, chod-l ullavva*
> *Tulli kalipava noti tulli kalipava.* (Kavi, 16)

> (*This white beauty sitting on my shoulders*
> *It's you, dear toddy*
> *White and gorgeous you are*
> *Gorgeous and tasty you are*
> *You dance and make us dance Bollavva*).

This is a song that describes the beauty of toddy in the midst of a discussion between demons and gods. This is a popular song even among those who may not know it was written by Appacha in his *Sree Kaaveri Naataka*. It is in such instances we see the playwright's localization. To include *bolle Kall* (toddy or white liquor) and its charms that effects all is one way of translating Kodava life, infusing it with practices that the author knew, knowing that this is not a scene in the Sanskrit Purana and which may not be approved of within the Brahminic ideology, Appacha's translation makes his plays transcend the spiritual and social excesses of Brahminism.

A scene describes a Dalit (referred to as Kembati Poleya, by the caste name) drinking the sacred Kaaveri water and being purged of all his sins (Kavi 42–46)—is an example of how salvation can be brought in by the vernacular to all. Citing Novetzke again: 'Vernacularization is not just literary, aesthetics, but signals a social change as well. This also had an effect on given culture and polity—and it is not only language that is available for vernacularization but also other expressive idioms [ … ]' (2016, 6). So, for Novetzke, critiquing Sheldon Pollock, vernacularization is not 'primarily about the creation of a new literature [ … ]. I argue that the emphasis on the everyday life compels a cultural politics, and that politics, in turn, engages two of the most salient features of thirteenth-century life in Maharastra, which are caste and gender' (2016, 34).

That Appacha wanted these excesses to be known among the myriad hierarchized communities of Kodagu and moves towards a cultural politics imagining a new social order is evident in another interesting scene. He describes a place where a Brahmin speaking in Kannada and two commoners speaking in Tulu and Kodava, all planning to attend Kaaveri's wedding with sage Agastya (Kavi, 71–76). It is interesting not just because Appacha is proficient in all these languages but also because he brings in three languages on the same page in one play. In the early twentieth century while languages like Kodava and Tulu had hardly begun to be written down, to bring such languages to print and performance needed courage and imagination of a new kind. It imagined a community that was changing for the better, changing differently, imagining an identity that had many possibilities. Unlike Chinnappa who uses English, Appacha acknowledges the contribution of these languages to his compilation and sees Kodavas as autonomous and sees possibilities for Kodavas within the realm of Kaaveri Purana. The characters in the ancient Sanskrit plays like those of Kalidaasa, spoke the language assigned to them by a caste hierarchy. Appacha seems to represent the people and their lived-languages that inhabit the Kodagu country in order for them to be aware of Kaaveri's spiritual prowess, an act as he mentions in his foreword that can reach one and all, irrespective of whether they are learned in Sanskrit or not. More significantly, Appacha uses these languages to destabilize Brahman and his Sanskrit. More of a reformist, Appacha saw these vernaculars as important to be vernacularized. Despite being modelled after Sanskrit, this vernacularization questions it and is a claim towards equality in acts of writing and of life.

In another scene of the *Kaaveri Naataka*, the River Kaaveri is enraged with her husband, the sage Agasthya who broke his promise to her. This makes Kaaveri flow away as a river in anger, leaving Agasthya for good. Agasthya is upset at the fact that a woman can leave him, the great sage, and asks some Brahmins and some Kodavas present there to settle the matter. Kodavas hesitate to talk in fear of Agasthya's famous temper and ask the Brahmins to negotiate first. The Brahmins mention the Kodava saying '*pattama padekaaga, peereke karikaaga*' (Kavi, 95) meaning 'Brahmins aren't meant for the battlefield and the ridge gourd is not meant for a curry', their duty being only around God's affairs and not to settle disputes among anyone. It is then the Kodavas speak on the aside and I translate a long passage.

> Look at these men talking? Their talk is always crooked ... They pushed our ancestors into a corner by saying 'if you learn to read and write, you will be born as a bull, if you learn to write your name, you will be childless', and so on. Why is this not applicable to those Brahmins who alone can learn the letters, can read the vedas, and the puranas. None of us are allowed to learn reading and writing. We should not scold them, beat them, or even touch them! The rest of us should plough, sow, work hard, and take the harvest first to these Brahmins and they should eat well ... which sinner made all these rules? These Brahmins made these rules that do not allow us to learn the letters so that their free food will not stop, so that their secrets will not be out [ ... ]. Whenever we have approached the Brahmin to teach us letters, they have fooled us. It was such a revelation to know from the *mutts* that any good human can be a Brahmin! (Kavi, 95–96)

Kodavas in the play (referred to as *deshakaara*, 'people of the country'), continue to say: 'we believed the Brahmins years ago and every village got a temple. If we continue that belief, each clan will have a temple' (104). Further: 'You can keep the gods you made to yourselves. We do not want their trouble. If you are going, take all your gods with you' (108).

The questions Appacha posed in his foreword and in his plays point to an identity that reclaims a past devoid of caste hierarchies while simultaneously envisioning a future for reading and writing aong the Kodavas. The questions are answered here within the story of the play and answered by Kodavas who now have the authority of the written word. These are not just anti-Brahminical statements, but dialogues that see the logic of caste and for us here, see the connection between caste and the act of writing. It wants to move beyond Sanskrit. If not anti-Sanskrit, it is clearly anti-Brahmanical. This is why Appacha chose to write and to write it in a manner that saw through the oppressive Brahminic logic. This reminds us of the parallel Hany Babu (2017) draws between the linguistic hierarchy and the caste system by invoking the notion of *chaturvarna* that posits Sanskrit as occupying a privileged position and other languages at hierarchized lower levels (Babu 2017, 113). The thought processes and the anti-caste logic are apparent. The gods are manufactured, caste is manufactured, reading and writing are banned so that the act of manufacturing remains a sacred secret, to protect Brahminical interests. Kodavas, as the characters claim, know how to live by toil, not by cheating everyone. This comment on the productive force of people as against that of the Brahman who lives on the labour of other echoes Kancha Ilaiah's (1996) notions of Dalitization (117–123).

## Conclusion

Christian Novetzke uses the idea of 'sonic equality', to describe the acts of early vernacularization in Marathi (2016). Sonic equality is characteristic of the compositions of Janadev and Chakradar in Marathi. These composers composed in Marathi, in a manner that women and lowered castes could understand and get closer to God, something that was not possible in esoteric Sanskrit. This idea is also applicable to Appacha and Appaiah, although the contexts are very different for the hill people, the Kodavas. Appacha's play was meant to be performed. It is not really meant to be read and Appaiah's work was meant to be critically read, situating Kodavas in an upwardly mobile world trying to figure a better-placed caste term for a people outside of the caste system. Chinnappa's work focused on the Kodava performative genres that needed to be reformed. By performance, the play and performative genres are not only a continuation of the performative traditions of the Kodava but also continues the democratic tradition by reaching out to whoever sees the play and/ or hears the play performed. It is not restricted to the world of letters inscribed. Like storytelling and dancing, it translates a world into another world that does not really require any prerequisite knowledge. This is why Appacha and Chinnappa and Appaiah are important. Through their translation of the Kodava and into Kodava, through their insertion of an anti-Brahmin logic to the word, they ushered in an era that brought the word into Kodava, which opened new worlds that could lead to questioning, acceptance, rejection, and a combination of many prevalent notions. Although Appaiah believed and represented Kodavas differently within the Hindu realm, that he too does not accept Brahminic literature unquestioningly puts him in this group of early Kodava writers.

As Choksi (2018) argues, by translating the orality to script, these early authors contest notions of identity at various levels. 'The assertion of orality as the primary feature of Adivasi life ... has displaced Adivasi practices onto the realm of "pure culture" ' (Choksi 2018, 92). Not only is the constantly changing orality of the community transformed in yet another way, but in a way that critiqued existing casteist practices of writing.

The three texts analysed, three early texts authored by Kodava men on Kodavas appear to be anxious, to make sense of their identity as Kodava in a rapidly changing world where writing becomes accessible to them. The anxiety and contradictions within these three texts suggest that there is indeed something 'different' about the Kodavas that needs to be sorted out, to be legitimized, to be placed in/out of contexts. Appaiah and Appacha worked within an environment of Hindu reform, while Chinnappa worked with the colonial, and this is reflected in how their ideas are translated into the written word. Although none of the translations are clear in their affiliation to one or the other written/dominant ideology, it is clear that their intention is to translate into Kodava, their intention is to translate Kodava as a culture, as an identity that demanded the dignity of the word, dignity of articulation, and dignity of translation. This is also significant since both literization (the very beginning of the act of writing), and literarization (the emergence of literature, both aesthetic and political)[9] seems to be emerging simultaneously and combined with a critique of Sanskrit literarization. This critique of the existing powerful caste-based religious literary system is definitely a translation of both 'modernity and pre-historicity' as Basnett shows (2006, 4), a translation that forged newer identities for an ethnolinguistic minority, an identity different from the colonizer, different from the privileged castes, and one that sought writing as a tool that would further propagate the rich orality cementing the indigenous autonomous identity of the Kodavas.

---

[9] See Sheldon Pollock's (2006) detailed discussion on literization and literarization in his *The Language of the Gods in the World of Men.*

# References

Asad, Talal. 1986. 'The Concept of Cultural Translation in British Social Anthropology'. In *Writing Culture: The Poetics and Politics of Ethnography*, eds James Clifford and George E. Marcus, pp. 141–164. Berkeley and Los Angeles, CA: University of California Press.

Babu, Hany. 2017. 'Breaking the Chaturvarna System of Languages The Need to Overhaul the Language Policy'. *Economic and Political Weekly* 52 (23): 112–119.

Basnett, Susan. 2006. 'Reflections on Comparative Literature in the Twenty-First Century'. *Comparative Critical Studies* 3 (1–2): 3–11.

Boldrini, Lucia. 2010. 'Comparative Literature and Translation, Historical Breaks and Continuing Debates: Can the Past Teach us Something about the Future?'. *Diacrítica. Dossier Literatura Comparada* 24 (3): 181–199.

Chandran, Mini. 2017. 'Dancing in a Hall of Mirrors: Translation between Indian Languages'. In *Multilingual Nation: Translation and Language Dynamics in India*, ed. Rita Kothari, pp. 273–290. New Delhi: Oxford University Press.

Choksi, Nishaant. 2018. 'Script as Constellation Among Munda Speakers: The Case of Santhali'. *South Asian History and Culture* 9 (1): 92–115.

Connor. Lt. P. 1870. *Memoirs of the Codugu Survey*. Bangalore: Central Jail Press.

Ganapathy, B. D. 1918 (2010). 'Introduction to the Poet'. In *Shree Kaaveri Naataka* from *Naal Naataka*, by Haradasa Appacha Kavi, pp. vi–xii. Madikeri: Karnataka Kodava Sahitya Akademi.

Ilaiah, Kancha. 1996. *Why I Am Not a Hindu: A Sudra Critique of Hindutva Philosophy, Culture and Political Economy*. Calcutta: Samya.

Kavi, Haradasa Appacha. 1918 (2010). *Shree Kaaveri Naataka* from *Naal Naataka*. Madikeri: Karnataka Kodava Sahitya Akademi.

Koravanda, Dr Appaiah. 1902 (2003). *Kodavara Kulaachaaradi Tatvajeevini* ('An Explication of Kodava Life and Customs'), trans. Theethira Rekha Vasanth. Madikeri: Karnataka Kodava Sahitya Akademi.

Moegling, Herman. 1855. *Coorg Memoirs: An Account of Coorg Memoirs and of the Coorg Mission*. Bangalore: Wesleyan Missionary Press.

Mukherjee, Sujit. 1994. 'Translation as New Writing'. In *Translation as Discovery*, pp. 77–85. New Delhi: Sangam Books.

Nadikerianda, Chinnappa. 1924. *Pattole Palame* ('Words on Silk'). Bengaluru: Kannada Pustaka Pradhikara.

Nadikerianda, Chinnappa (trans. by Bovverianda Nanjamma and Chinnappa). 2003 [1924]. *Pattole palame* [Words on silk]. New Delhi: Rupa.

Nair, Janaki. 2012. *Mysore Modern: Rethinking the Region Under Princely Rule*. Hyderabad: Orient Blackswan.

Niranjana, Tejaswini. 1992. *Siting Translation: History, Post-structuralism, and the Colonial Context*. Berkeley, CA: University of California Press.

Novetzke, Christian. 2016. *The Quotidian Revolution: Vernacularization, Religion, and the Pre-modern Public Sphere in India*. New York: Columbia University Press.

Novetzke, Christian Lee. 2018. 'Religion and Public Sphere in Premodern India'. *ASIA* 72 (1): 147–176.

Pollock, Sheldon. 2006. *The Language of the Gods in the World of Men*. New Delhi: Permanent Black.

Ramanujan, A. K. 1991. 'Three Hundred Rāmāyaṇas: Five Examples and Three Thoughts on Translation'. In *Many Rāmāyaṇas: The Diversity of a Narrative Tradition in South Asia*, ed. Paula Richman, pp. 22–48. Berkeley, CA: University of California Press.

Rice, Lewis. 1878. *Mysore and Coorg: A Gazetteer*. Bangalore: Mysore Government Press.

Richter, G. 1870. *Gazetteer of Coorg*. New Delhi: Low Price Publications.

Said, Edward. 1978. *Orientalism*. New York: Pantheon Books.

Scott, James. 2009. *The Art of Being Governed. An Anarchist History of Upland Southeast Asia*. Hyderabad: Orient Blackswan.

# 3

# For English and for Tongues, Our Own

This chapter begins with two issues around English that created quite a flutter in 2021. Sometime in April 2021, a video went viral that showed a professor from the Indian Institute of Technology, Kharagpur, violently abusing students belonging to Dalit and Bahujan castes and other minorities. The professor concerned was subsequently suspended[1] and many have written and commented on the casteist nature of our society that is continuously manifested in our higher education institutions (HEIs). What is relevant to the language debate here is that much of these expressions of casteist brutalities in HEIs happen in the realm of merit and the English language. It is in one such 'English remedial class' where the Scheduled Castes, Scheduled Tribes and the Other Backward Classes (SC/ST/OBC) students aspiring to study at the Indian Institute of Technology but whose English required *remedy* and were abused. This simultaneity of aspiration for higher education in English and the dominant's perception of remedy for such aspirations is a story so complex that unpacking it needs nuances that we are little equipped with. Thirumal, commenting on this issue mentions how 'modern secular education in post-independence India has displayed its inability to replace caste as an institution for building "character" in terms of the capacity of living with' (2021, 15).

If the above is in the context of HEIs, the following is in the context of high school education. The Central Board of Secondary Education (CBSE) of India, a board that oversees education at the central level, conducted tenth grade exams for CBSE students in December 2021. The English exam had a comprehension passage with sentences like 'emancipation of women destroyed the parent's authority over the children' and 'it was only by accepting her husband's way that a mother could gain

[1] https://indianexpress.com/article/education/cbse-class-10-english-paper-receives-backlash-for-alleged-gender-stereotyping-cbse-issues-official-statement-7669795/

*Languages of Minority.* Sowmya Dechamma CC, Oxford University Press. © Oxford University Press 2024.
DOI: 10.1093/oso/9780198908456.003.0004

obedience over the younger ones', among others.[2] After ruffled parents stirred this up, the issue became political. Eventually the CBSE released a notification saying that students would be getting full marks for this controversial passage which was not set as per the guidelines.[3] The question for us is obvious. Why is English a suitable discipline to bring in ideas of equality or here in this case, critique ideals of equality as disrupting familial harmony and concomitant tradition? Why does English lend itself to the discourse of a modernity that is perceived undesirable to a dominant section of society? If in the Indian Institute of Technology case it is the category of lowered caste of all genders seen as desiring English towards change but is considered unworthy by the very Western-inspired institution; in the case of the CBSE, it is gender whose changing dynamics (courtesy of feminism, a Western import, supposedly) that is seen as undesirable. English thus is seen as a harbinger of change, of modernity (however perceived), and also as something that disturbs the status quo of casteist–gendered society while simultaneously making it worthwhile for the heretofore worthy categories of select caste and gendered populace.

This contradictory nature of English that is at once alien to the context of caste but also is dear to people, precisely because it lacks a memory of caste, is evocatively articulated by Rita Kothari in the context of Dalit writing and translation into English:

> despite the fact that trenchantly local realities and registers of caste are difficult to couch in a language that has no memory of caste [ ... ], English promises to Dalit writers (at least in theory), as both individuals and (however problematically) as representatives of communities, agency, articulation, recognition, and justice. (2013, 61)

Arguing how this 'castelessness' of English is indeed a strength and not inadequacy, Kothari points to how the hegemony of standardized languages of India is a burden upon Dalits and Dalit writers who are seen as speakers of dialects that are undesirable, impure. It is precisely because English is alien and global that it is empowering, freeing minorities from

---

[2] https://www.indiatoday.in/education-today/news/story/cbse-class-10-english-paper-controversial-topic-to-fetch-students-full-marks-1887252-2021-12-13
[3] https://www.indiatoday.in/education-today/news/story/cbse-class-10-english-paper-controversial-topic-to-fetch-students-full-marks-1887252-2021-12-13

the clutches of standardized Gujarathi or Kannada enmeshed with local politics of caste, identity, and language. English, thus holding both material and symbolic power, allows Dalits to use it as a foster tongue, while 'mother tongue' has become a claimant of upper-caste's sophisticated standards.

Public education is a matter under the purview of individual states in India and most states impart school education in the dominant language of the region. The central government's education is imparted in Hindi (or/and in English in schools like Kendriya Vidyalaya and Jawahar Navodaya Vidyalaya). Given that it is the under-privileged who are in the public education system, English education offered in a range of private schools are accessible only to those who can afford it, most often than not belonging to the privileged castes. But this does not discount the crucial role English plays. Consider, for example, the Roman script that came to us via English being used as the script by most languages in the Northeast of India (be it Khasi, Ao, Lotha, Mizo, or for that matter Konkani and Santali, in some cases), to write, acquire knowledge in newer ways combined with the knowledge systems current in the language culture. While most of the languages of the Northeast are today written in the Roman script, Bodo, the language of the Bodo people from Assam was not 'granted permission'[4] to use the Roman script and instead had to make do with the Devanagari script. That most other Northeastern states are predominantly Christian and indigenous/tribal, but Assam where Bodo is situated is largely Hindu/neo-Hindu might have influenced this is anybody's guess. As I have discussed in the earlier chapters, this connection of script to the identity of a language and people is largely a phenomenon in the Indian subcontinent despite many of the Indo-Aryan languages written in Devanagari script or modified versions of it. Here then, we see how language, script, and community are tightly interwoven into notions of identity. English suggests, means, and has real consequences in the lives all of us lead today. From languages in India using the Roman script, to the building of a temple for the English goddess; to the proliferation of translated works into English from various languages of India; to the manner in which kids are herded into relatively cheaper English-medium schools, English's centrality in our lives is unparalleled.

[4] From *The Bodos: A Revolutionary Journey* (6).

English is also crucial to the ways in which the IT sector has transformed our language, knowledge, and mobility. The coming of social media has changed language usage where even dominant Indian languages with a history of script also use Roman script.—In this complex scenario, how have different minorities expressed their aspiration for English as a language and for English education bestowed to us by the English colonizer is the question this chapter attempts to address.

Since the times of Thomas Babington Macaulay whose contempt for anything other than certain European languages and literature, to the times when the letter (to be analysed a little later here) written by Kodava clan heads seeking English education for boys and girls, and to the present where a temple is built for the English Goddess by Dalits in the remote village Banka in Uttar Pradesh, English has journeyed long, winding ways in the subcontinent. Tharakeshwar traces this journey of English thus:

> The question of English was invariably tied with the question of India as a nation. If Dalit politics had to address certain issues of a pan-Indian nature in the 1990s and 2000s, it had to be pan-Indian, and could not remain linguistic-state oriented. English as a signifier of the (Indian) nation (or the Union) had come to the fore. English also gave Dalit issues visibility at the international level, as evident during the Durban conference; and now it is a major issue in American academics, propelling translations and publications from foreign universities. (2014, 172)

As a language initially taken over by the nationalist elites of the subcontinent whom Sudipta Kaviraj and Paul Brass term as 'bilingual elites', English soon began to be perceived as the only language that could potentially liberate the oppressed castes, because English did not merely suggest a language as the Indian Institute of Technology Kharagpur and CBSE issues showcased earlier. It suggested a new world that brought with it a mobility, a modernity that theoretically at least had visions of 'liberty, equality, and fraternity', especially through the education the English rule made available to people of all genders and castes. This is even more crucial in the subcontinent because the language of the gods, Sanskrit, was also the main language of knowledge—a language that only the upper-caste male could access.

Further, drawing from Tharakeshwar again:

> only when the state jobs started shrinking and the number of educated
> Dalits began increasing—a situation that pushed Dalits to seek jobs in
> the private sector/service sector, which was expanding rapidly—did
> the question of English become important to the Dalit movement.
> (2014, 170)

## English Aspiration and Dalit–Bahujan Narratives

Not just the gods' language but since practices of writing and reading
that were in vogue in the dominant vernaculars for the longest time were
also accessible only to the same minutest section of the society, English
brought with it an aspiration that went beyond practices of reading and
writing. In this context where religious, ritual, knowledge, and the language complex is closely tied to hierarchies, how have women of all
castes, people of backward castes, Dalits, and ethnolinguistic minorities
perceived English? Arguing for an education system that enables learning
both in English and in the language spoken by the child at home, Kancha
Ilaiah, unlike most scholars of language, sees the role of English as equally
significant as the language spoken at home in a child's cognitive and social development. His anecdote quoted below says a hundred things:

> One bright morning in 1960, when I was about eight, a newly appointed
> teacher came to my house. My mother had already cleaned our court-
> yard, or 'vaakili', and was sprinkling dung water all around. I was about
> to assist my elder brother in untying cattle and going along with them
> for grazing. The teacher asked my mother to send me and my elder
> brother, who was about 10, to school. What she told him shocks every
> one of us in retrospect: 'Ayyaa—if we send our children to school to
> read and write, the devil Saraswathi will kill them. That devil wants only
> Brahmins and baniyas to be in that business'. (2)

Note the daily routine of the family that revolves around cleaning
the courtyard, untying and grazing the cattle, and the involvement
of everyone in the house in labouring for the livelihood of the family.

These early mornings are busy with required chores that are productive unlike the 'devil's business' of reading and writing that have no immediate value to livelihood. This devil's business is not just non-productive but also might bring harm to Dalit–Bahujan children whose limits are set by conventions. Saraswati, the upper-caste Hindu goddess of knowledge and arts thus becomes a devil in Ilaiah's mother's view. It is here that we need to locate the contradictory journeys English has taken over the last two centuries in the Indian subcontinent. The introduction to *English in the Dalit Context* charts how 'Dalits neither accept nor aspire for English unconditionally' (Rani 2017, 3) but it is a debate that cannot be set aside on lines of what Susie Tharu says (1998, 27) in her *Subject to Change*. That English works with the potential of both reformist and radical frameworks is illustrated by Suneetha Rani by invoking the example of Cornelia Sorabjee, who could 'access English education and went on to become a lawyer but was not allowed to enroll in the bar council for 20 years for being a woman' (Rani 2017, xv). One also has to take into consideration that be it nationalist or imperialist reform, the focus of both was largely on 'the privileged woman (the normative family woman)' (xxi). Although this chapter takes a different perspective on the imperialist reform, there is much to agree with Suneetha Rani's proposition that 'English became an agency for women to express themselves and to explore the domains of knowledge that they were not allowed to access earlier' (xxiii). Prem Poddar's observations that there is little or no difference in the manner imperialism used it and nationalism used it is quite crucial:

> The reason why political independence has not 'freed' the discipline of English studies from its colonial moorings has partly to do with the nature of colonialism's other: nationalism. The fact is that the discourse of nationalism, despite its overt antipathy to alien rule, shared many of the same epistemological and axiological assumptions which motivated the colonial enterprise. (quoted in Alok Mukherjee, 2009, 248)

To epistemological and axiological we might as well add 'political' in quotes. For the nationalist mission almost replicated the same missionary zeal, the burden to civilize without working towards structural changes in the society, the opposition to the Hindu Code Bill immediately after Indian independence being a significant case in point.[5] Mukherjee writes: 'the writings and actions of Dr. Ambedkar, in particular, suggest an early understanding of the possibilities of emancipation presented by English through access to western knowledge and, thereby a particular sensibility' (290). In a similar vein, Rita Kothari mentions how Dalit texts translated into the English sphere acquire a new representation, new identity, and how translation into English gives the texts and the authors a platform to overcome local politics that usually dismisses any Dalit writing. Interestingly, Kothari argues how this independence that English provides is a result of its lack of memory of caste which simultaneously generates awareness about caste among an international audience (2013, 62). It is this complex connection of English with caste that is liberating despite the hurdles that make it difficult for Dalit–Bahujans and most sections of the minorities to access English is reiterated by Anand:

> [B]rahmanical elite during the nationalist movement and in the immediate post-independence phase held a tight English leash over the institutions of power/knowledge. But one has to acknowledge the fact that (western/colonial) 'modernity' that comes with English is something that is not inaccessible to the 'untouchables'—the Dalits and Bahujans whose marginalization has been justified over centuries by dominant varieties of Hinduism. (1999, 2053)

Ambedkar, of course is the significant example to turn to for inspiration. In his work 'Who were the Shudras?' written in 1946, Ambedkar wrote so very pointedly about research in Indian society. One of the first questions he begins with is the question of language; the question of who has the right to write and in what language. Bear with this long quote from Ambedkar:

> I have already been warned that while I may have a right to speak on Indian politics, religion and religious history of India are not my field and that I must not enter it. [ ... ] I am ready to admit that I am not

---

[5] Ambedkar's and Tagore's critiques of the nation and how social reform need to be prioritized over political reform is illuminating.

competent to speak even on Indian politics. If the warning is for the reason that I cannot claim mastery over the Sanskrit language, I admit this deficiency. But I do not see why it should disqualify me altogether from operating in this field. There is very little of literature in the Sanskrit language which is not available in English. The want of knowledge of Sanskrit need not therefore be a bar to my handling a theme such as the present. For I venture to say that a study of the relevant literature, albeit in English translations, for 15 years ought to be enough to invest even a person endowed with such moderate intelligence like myself, with sufficient degree of competence for the task. (1946/2002: 387)

What does Ambedkar mean here? One, until 1946 whoever studied, commented, and wrote on Hindu society were men who knew Sanskrit clearly implying that these were Brahmin men. Ambedkar also very clearly points that the knowledge of Hindu society is not dependent on Sanskrit! It can be done in English (and in lived experiences) that have become more accessible to Dalits and Shudras than Sanskrit. Two, and more importantly, this knowledge of Hindu society coming from non-Sanskritic foundations has to be considered equally or more seriously than Sanskrit-based knowledge. (This place perhaps ironically is being taken by English today as Hany Babu argues.) Carrying forward the argument made in the last two chapters, translation stands here as the most authentic and also as the most accessible form that is also a harbinger of knowledge, while simultaneously breaking the boundaries of caste-restricted knowledge. Sanskrit and English do not just remain languages in this discourse but are trapped in the structures of knowledge and power within social relations. This endows both Sanskrit and English with a sensibility that has been perceived in a spectrum of ideologies, including the one Ambedkar was part of as Kothari argues.

Considering how Ambedkar was himself formed in considerable measure by liberal thought and systemic understanding of caste, which he acquired in the course of his education in the west, English played a constitutive role in his life. Without undermining the experiential discrimination he underwent, it may be possible to say that not only did Ambedkar create something through English, but that he was himself also a creation of English. Ambedkar set in motion a political language of rights, as well as practices of self-expression and narratives. (Kothari 2013, 63)

To English perhaps we can attribute Ambedkar's pan-Indianness, a criteria that anti-caste reformers like Periyar, Iyothee Thass, Sri Narayana Guru, and Ayyankali would have greatly benefited from.

English education and English's collaboration with Christianity and colonialism is a foregone conclusion as many scholars[6] have pointed out. And as mentioned, it has travelled, and is travelling across times, across continents, in very many ways, often in conflicting ways. Alok Mukherjee maps these travels succinctly:

English was initially sought by 'high' caste Hindus as an instrument of revival, and while in post-independence India it was expected to serve the dominant group as a pipeline for communication within and a window without, now, groups that have been historically oppressed and disenfranchised, in particular, the Dalits, are looking to English as a means for emancipation and empowerment. (Mukherjee 2009, 312)

One can perhaps therefore safely assume that 'English' has had different ramifications for different communities. The anxiety of cultural loss connected with losing one's superior ritual and political status was not a concern for the minoritized as differences in the early Malayalam novels written by lowered castes and privileged castes show. *Saraswativijayam* written by Potheri Kunhambu in 1892, has as its epitaph 'Education is the greatest wealth'. Analysing this novel, Dilip Menon writes: 'education was not just an abstract formulation, a hope in the promise of mobility through knowledge' (1892, 121). Needless to add, this education was a 'gift' of English to the oppressed castes as Savitribai Phule's poems from the mid-nineteenth century make evident.

> Manu-follower Peshwas are dead and gone
> Manu's the one who barred us from education.
> Givers of knowledge—the English have come
> Learn, you've had no chance in a millennium.

[6] Gauri Viswanathan, Rajeshwari Sunder Rajan (1992); Svati Joshi (1991).

> We'll teach our children and ourselves to learn
> Receive knowledge, become wise to discern.
> [ ... ] Awake, arise and educate
> Smash traditions—liberate![7]

The poem is self-evident. Also evident is the nature of history, the awareness of history, and what it has done to most, resulting in a call to capture the moment of English's arrival. For both Potheri Kunhambu and Savitribai Phule, writing in entirely different locations, different languages, and likely not being aware of each other, English moves beyond the realm of language and offers itself as a metanarrative that is potentially transformative of their individual and community selves. They wrote in Malayalam and Marathi, for English education. At a time when writing in any language including in one's own was in itself liberative, writing for English in one's language in a caste-ridden public sphere points to the metaliberating effect and affect of English. What is also important for us is this—at a time when nationalist fervour was growing in mid- and late nineteenth century, people from the oppressed castes across the subcontinent did not subscribe to the dominant nationalist perspective that was framed within an anti-colonial paradigm by positing a spiritual self alongside a militant superiority over the materially painted colonizer. Kunhambu and Savitribai Phule break down the mysticism and assumed superiority of this spirituality of the dominant caste. Their understanding of education blurs the distinction between materiality and spirituality. It is education that will liberate spiritually and materially too. What these writings showcase is the difference in ideology from the privileged castes who held their culture and spirituality closely guarded by giving 'no chance in a millennium' for the lowered castes to be educated. This couching of the materiality of education and social capital of the dominant castes in the name of spirituality and culture is laid bare by thinkers like Kunhambu and Savitribai.

While not dismissing the role of English in cementing the authority of elite castes in the manner of access to education, law, and other colonial apparatus, Pandian argues that:

---

[7] https://drambedkarbooks.com/2015/01/03/few-poems-by-savitribai-phule/. Accessed 13 November 2021.

[...] if we foreground dominant nationalism in an oppositional dia-
logue with the subaltern social groups within the nation—instead of
colonialism—the divide between the spiritual and material, inner and
outer, would tell us other stories—stories of domination and exclusion
under the sign of culture and spirituality within the so-called national
community itself. (2002: 1736)

Also note another difference. Popular and known nationalist writers like
Bankim Chandra Chatterjee who initially wrote in English, switched to
writing in their tongue (Bangla in this case), asserting an identity expressed via 'one's own', nevertheless continuing in the British administrative system and even tempering down ideas against Britain in subsequent
versions of *Anandamath*.[8]

Mainstream nationalists like Chatterjee for whom English was only a
'material' necessity expressed thus:

Unless the English rule, it will not be possible for the Eternal Code
to be reinstated. [ ... ] For a long time now the outward knowledge
has been lost in this land, and so the true Eternal Code has been lost
too. [ ... ] The outward knowledge no longer exists in this land, and
there's no one to teach it; we ourselves are not good at teaching people
such things. So we must bring in the outward knowledge from another country. The English are very knowledgeable in the outward
knowledge, and they're very good at instructing people. Therefore
we'll make them king. And when by this teaching our people are well
instructed about external things, they'll be ready to understand the
inner. (Chatterjee 1882, 229)

English was a necessary evil until one's own eternal spiritual code was
realized and reinstated. But for Savitribai Phule and Kunjambu, it was the
opposite. The cultural and social usurpation of Sanskrit's caste structured
ideals could only be overcome by English. I wish to add here a note of
caution and a note of explanation. This presumed spirituality of Sanksrit
is not to point to its non-materiality. Sanskrit and its attendant ideals and

---

[8] Julius Lipner, 2005 (1882). 'Introduction' to Bankim Chatterjee's, *Anandamath* or *The Sacred
Brotherhood*.

practices were indeed very material.[9] It begot the best material benefits to a select few. What follows is also that the realm of English was not limited to the world of the material but also spiritual in the sense that it is up-lifting, enabling, a language which allowed one to dream, to move beyond the restrictions for which one was not responsible.

English's spirituality therefore needs to be located in the democratic ideals that it perhaps unwittingly carried into the caste structures of India—the coming equality, liberty, and fraternity via English, via English language and literature, and also via English, the colonizer. Intellectual and knowledge ideals merged with the ideals of equality. As we now know, the first two were and are largely used by the privileged castes, while the ideals of the intellectual and equality were embraced by Dalit–Bahujan intellectuals like Phules and Ambedkar. It is here that the dominant nationalist discourse which frames itself largely within an anti-colonialist lens, falls short.

## Desiring English

Here is yet another example of how people outside the caste Hindu fold viewed the coming of English education. This is a letter written in 1862 by clan heads of the Kodava community from Kodagu/Coorg in Karnataka to officials in the British government. This letter is reproduced in the Public Instruction Reports of Coorg, compiled and written by Lewis Rice in 1882. This is also another story that gives us more to think about the different roles English plays in our lives.

> We, the undersigned headmen of Coorg, being the representatives of our countrymen, beg most respectfully to lay before you what is now uppermost in our minds, and what appears to us of the greatest importance for the welfare of our people.
>
> Through the noble generosity of the late lamented Chief Commissioner, General Sir Mark Cubbon, KCB, the blessing of

---

[9] A. K. Ramanujan in his 'Is there an Indian Way of Thinking?', convincingly argues how the context-sensitive nature of caste-ridden Hindu society is actually more materialistic than spiritual (57).

education has been extended to us six years ago, though at the time we did not appreciate as to its possible effect. But the influence of the established English school at Mercara, its steady progress, the temperate, judicious, and devoted manner in which it has been carried on for the last six years, together with the encouragement from the successive Superintendents, have disarmed all our fears, and we most earnestly desire that all our children should be benefited by the instruction there given.

The great influx of European settlers into our country makes the education of our children appear doubly necessary to our minds, since our own ignorance renders our intercourse with the planters most difficult, unsatisfactory and disadvantageous.

The peculiar circumstance, however, that Mercara, though the principal town contains but a few Coorg houses, enables only a limited number of Coorg boys to attend the school. To remedy this disadvantage, we have resolved to collect amongst ourselves a sum of money sufficient to build and endow a boarding house for about one hundred boys. The Coorg officials and pensioners are ready to contribute half a month's pay, which, together with the subscription of the farmers, will amount to about Rs. 6,000/-. This is all we can do for the present, but we earnestly wish that our daughters should also receive some education, and for them we would have to build a similar house.

Mr. Richter, the present headmaster of the Anglo-vernacular school, who has conducted it for the last six years and our entire confidence, has not only given the first impulse to this movement, but declares himself with his esteemed partner most willing to carry out the proposed plans; and as they have hitherto acted as father and mother towards our children, we have not the least hesitation in confiding them also for the future to their paternal care. The inner arrangements of the boarding-houses, however, would be managed by our own people. (Rice, 1882, 4–5)

How do we understand this letter written in August 1862, at a time when most of mainstream India was warming to anti-colonial rhetoric, post-1857? Kodagu, now in Karnataka, known as Coorg in its anglicized version, was annexed by the British as a separate province under the Madras Presidency by a proclamation dated 7 May 1834.

The state of the government and missionary schools until 1857 left much to be desired with hardly any instructors and very little pay for existing instructors. It was only after the new scheme of education in 1857 that some semblance of regularity came into being. These efforts were spurred by the letter written and signed by more than fifty headmen of Coorg quoted above. Why at a time (in mid- to late nineteenth century) when English education even to boys was questioned by mainstream nationalists such as Ishwar Chandra Vidya Sagar, Bankim Chandra Chattopadhyaya, and Swami Vivekananda (Pani and Pattnaik, 2006, 59), but also pushed by anglicists like Raja Ram Mohan Roy, Coorgs/ Kodavas as a community came forward willingly to educate their sons and notably their daughters. The letter by the headmen is of course ambiguous and yet there is clarity on what should be the future course of English and English education in Coorg. It is written by clanhead *men* in a society that is not exactly patriarchal. It talks about the 'countrymen' referring to the Kodava/Coorg community as belonging to a country (Kodava *naad* or Kodag *desha* would be an equivalent term in Kodava language) and about the 'welfare' of its people through the new education. It mentions the initial hesitation that is 'disarmed' and now Kodavas are earnest in their 'desire' for English education for, it is a blessing. What is also interesting to note is that the school is also seen as an extension of family life, that is not really dissociated from the practices of the people but also necessary for the new economy that has brought in coffee plantations via the English. This combining of the 'inner-family' with that of the inevitable change in the economy becomes interesting since the headmendo not really harp on a past culture/practice but are able to see the future from various standpoints. It is not a letter that accepts English uncritically, but accepts it on its own terms, strategically, over and above Kannada that was the language of the Lingayat rulers for about two hundred years, and also during the British rule, to which very minute numbers had access and in which Kodavas had no say whatsoever.

Similar to what Ilaiah and Phule argue, this system of education worked differently for different communities and genders. How was progress understood in relation to English education? How can we understand this within or beyond the framework of colonial modernity and anti-colonial nationalism? What notions of gender and community did

English education inscribe into the existing ones of the community? What does this tell us about English in general?

In forwarding the petition written by the clan heads, the superintendent and the commissioner of Mysore and Coorg wrote very supportively, obviously tinted with 'orientalist' notions: 'I beg to bear testimony to the genuineness of the people to progress in knowledge, their readiness to make sacrifices in the cause', wrote Captain Campbell, the superintendent (Rice 1882, 4–5). The Commissioner, Mr Bowring, wrote:

> It has rarely happened in India that a whole race has come forward in this manner, putting aside traditional prejudices, to meet half-way the earnest wish of their rulers that they should educate themselves, and it is especially remarkable among mountaineers in this country, as the hill races are generally far below those of the plains in their acquisition of knowledge. (Rice 1882, 4–5)

After these petitions and recommendations, Kolovanda Kariyappa, who was the first pupil to enrol in the Mercara English school in 1856 (then against the wishes of the headmen) offered to build the girls' boarding house at his own expense. Subsequently, many anglo–vernacular schools were started across Coorg to act as feeders to the Mercara school (Rice 1882, 2). Tejaswini Niranjana in her 'Translation, Colonialism and the Rise of English' argues how the introduction of English and the desire for English as portrayed by the colonizer cannot be separated from the subjection and subjectification. Using the examples from Charles Trevelyan and others, Niranjana elaborates on how Indians are represented as willingly submitting to power and desirous of colonial knowledge, desirous of English—all willingly.

> The introduction of English education in India is inextricable from the process of subjection/subjectification under colonialism. The colonial 'subject', constructed through practices or technologies of power/knowledge, participates willingly, [ … ], in his/her insertion into the dominant order. (Niranjana 1990, 773)

Does this letter then, written by clan heads of Kodava community, the poems written by Savitribai Phule around the same time, say other things

about 'willingness'? Can all willingness be forced? How do we understand the agency of the colonized, especially when articulating concerns
of the colonized who could seek privileged knowledge only with the
coming of English? The focus of scholars like Tejaswini Niranjana and
Gauri Vishwanathan is the writing, representation, and translation by the
colonizer. It is only when we bring in life stories from women and those
of lowered castes, indigenous communities that these narratives change
their course, most drastically.

Some more details from the Public Instruction Reports on Coorg
help us understand the changes that were brought in by the introduction of English, especially with regards to gender and community questions. Around 1875, an attempt was made to start a boarding school
under a European mistress but only day scholars could be obtained
and the mistress fell ill and resigned, ending the efforts for an all-girls
school. But as the records (Rice 1882, 12) show, girls continued to go
to mixed schools. Special schools were opened for Muslims in 1872.
In 1877, education for coolies of coffee estates were enquired into
and Coorg Planters' Association (constituting only British planters)
favoured it. But Coorgs were against opening schools for Holeyas (then
called untouchables) and jungle Tribes (Adivasis) given their 'no set-
tled status and no land to cultivate and given their wandering nature,'
again replicating denial of structures of access to people further down
in the societal structure. Over a period of a decade, English education
had made immense changes in the public sphere of colonial education
that brought in children of various genders, castes, and communities
into the realm of English. The *Report* mentions that the girls went to the
same schools as their brothers and relatives, passed through the same
classes and courses of study and generally remained unmarried to a
later age than is common among Hindus (Public Instruction Report
1882, 17). It is worthwhile to mention the paradox that the school
that was exclusively established for the girls in 1872 didn't have many
takers. But most schools that were not really intended to be mixed
gender schools ended up having girls as pupils. It should also be noted
that in Victorian England then, there were hardly any mixed schools.
This is also true for schools meant for untouchables. The small number
of lower castes who went to school, went to 'regular' schools and not

schools that were exclusively meant for them. In 1882, out of 21,000 children of school age, nearly 4000 went to school. This included children belonging to different communities and castes. It is very pertinent for us to note that there is no upper-caste group present in the data compiled by the Public Instruction Report, meaning their total population was negligible in the province. As we saw, there are numbers that indicate women, children of indigenous communities belonging to different orders of social hierarchies, people of 'untouchable' castes, and of minorities. There is a quote from the section of the Rice report titled 'Female Education':

> Female education so far as the Coorgs are concerned, presents fewer difficulties than in many parts of India, owing to the absence of prejudice on the subject and the later age at which girls are married. The attendance of so many girls in the boys' schools is an exceptional and pleasing feature, and exerts, it is believed, a good influence. (Rice, 1882, 17)

Most boys belonging to the Coorg community and a sixth of the girls from the community were attending school by 1882 when Lewis Rice wrote the report. This phenomenon has to be understood beyond the paradigm of reform prevalent in the late nineteenth century and beyond the paradigm of the civilizational burden of the colonizer. As argued, it can only be located in the already existing hierarchies in the society where written knowledge was seen as liberating, not just for the individual but also for gendered and communitarian categories. In addition, the gendered practices in these communities in their day-to-day practices always already were different from the casteist-gender practices of the dominant. With the coming of English, the social realm of interaction amongst people belonging to different communities saw, like elsewhere, a drastic change where children of various genders, castes, communities, religions could for the first time share a single space, inching slowly towards the idea of political–secular democracy that 'English' brought with it. This is an idea that is still in the making.

What was formal, written education in Coorg/Kodagu prior to the British is a question restricted to the royals and the Brahmins who came with them. These were Kannada and Tulu-speaking outsiders to the region. Literacy in Kannada and perhaps a little bit of Sanskrit was limited in the sense of what was considered essential and privileged knowledge of accounts and revenue-keeping and Hindu religious necessities (to which most communities in Kodagu did not belong) and needless to say, restricted to the male of royal privilege and Brahmin on lines with what James Scott tells us:

> Literacy in premodern societies was, under the best of circumstances, confined to a minuscule portion of the population, almost certainly less than 1 percent. It was the social property of scribes, accomplished religious figures, and a very thin stratum of scholar gentry. (2009, 224)

If this was the sphere of education that required the special skills of reading and writing, a glance at the Public Instruction reports says more: a total of 946 students were in the rolls in different schools of Coorg from 1834 to 1865 when the first report of Public instruction came out in 1867.[10] The total population of people belonging to all religions was 168,312.[11] This means, in 1867, after nearly two decades of formal colonial schooling, the percentage of literates was 0.56 per cent of the total population, assuming all who went to school became literate. One can imagine this number prior to 1834, before the setting up of formal education in Coorg. This, I think, can be safely assumed to be the pattern of literacy all over India prior to the establishment of colonial/missionary education. I wish to distinguish literacy and knowledge in the written from knowledge in all its forms and how at no time in history including our times (except in cases of orl-vedic times as discussed in the introduction), knowledge of reading and writing is the usually the only one that has been assigned value. Productive labour has never been 'useful/worthy' of knowledge and the idea of merit therefore has been skewed towards elite written knowledge.

---

[10] Report on Public Instruction in Coorg, 1867. Mysore Government Press, Bangalore, 25.

[11] Report on the Coorg General Census of 1871. Major A. W. C. Lindsay. Mysore Government Press, Bangalore, 3. As an interesting aside, the report classifies Coorgs (or Kodavas) as Coorgs and 'other Hindus' in another column, thus differentiating the Coorgs from Hindus, a practice that can be traced to the many colonial ethnographical writings that clearly saw Coorgs as outside the Hindu.

## Towards a Modernity: Ushered in by English

Here then, is a modernity ushered in by English education, literally speaking, the education brought in by the English. The 'literate' subjects did not necessarily learn/study in English. English was taught as a language except in a couple of schools where it was the medium of instruction. The schools mainly offered instruction in Kannada (known as Canarese) and to a small extent in 'Hindustani', aimed mostly at educating the Muslims. Noticeable is the absence of Sanskrit.

How do we understand modernities, aspirations, through English, through the subject of female education from poems (by Savitribai Phule), letters, and also from life stories that are not written down? The task and methods are not easy, especially because this work does not look into narratives by women but looks into the letter written by head men belonging to the community and records kept by the colonizer. The women here were not anglophiles, they were not elite, were not educated nor had access (and did not require this access) to the power of knowledge as framed by the British or by the Brahmins. A small section of Kodava women might have been daughters of well-to-do farmers but we have no access whatsoever to their own stories.[12] Their stories and narratives are mediated through men of the community to some extent and largely by the colonial official, record-keeper, ethnographer, and, of course, memories and lives narrated to people around them, and folk lores which is beyond the focus here.

Unlike the nationalists in other places who had to work against the idea of oriental decadence to build a superior culture of their own, making women central to their nationalist scheme of things, for ethnolinguistic indigenous communities like the Kodava and for the backward and lowered castes, the burden of proving—'our tradition was great'—simply never existed. In a culture where tradition was embedded with the materiality of existence connected to the spirituality of here and now, tracing a past that was superior to that of the British, and to preserve that past despite its encounter with newer ways brought in by the British—was an

---

[12] See Veena Poonacha's study *From the Land of a Thousand Hills: Portraits of Three Kodagu Women* (2002) which traces the life stories and aspirations of three generations of women from her family who had begun to get formal education starting from the early twentieth century.

anxiety (which Pandian has brilliantly articulated) that did not exist for communities outside the nationalist elite castes. English was central in breaking this material and spiritual anxiety as Pandian's analysis shows:

> The very domain of sovereignty that nationalism carves out in the face of colonial domination is simultaneously a domain of enforcing domination over the subaltern social groups such as lower castes, women and marginal linguistic regions, by the national elite. For example, Partha Chatterjee, in discussing Tarinicharan Chattopadhayay's *The History of India*, notes, 'If the 19th century Englishman could claim ancient Greece as his classical heritage, why should not the English-educated Bengali feel proud of the achievement of the so-called Vedic civilisation?' [ ... ] The nationalist invocation of Vedic civilisation indeed challenges the claims to supremacy by the colonisers. However, it also carries an unstated hierarchisation of different social groups that go to make the nation. The normativity of a Vedic civilisation, reinvented by dominant nationalism, would accommodate vast sections of Indians only as inferiors within the nation. (Pandian 2002, 1736)

These dominant versions of what is assumed to be Indian culture conflated with nationalisms are countered by Pandian using contemporary examples. When we begin to look at narratives that are few but never made visible like that of the letter we saw and writings by Phule, Muktabai Salve, Corenelia Sorabjee, and Ambedkar, we see that girls from all castes (and their families) and men from many castes sought education almost with a vengeance. What is noteworthy is that the critique against English in Bengal in the mid- and late nineteenth century and other regions of cultural power came from within the circle of the elite English speakers. From among the outliers of caste, the critique was at least visibly absent and support for English education came from within the community, people who were not established in colonial service. The tension as we saw in the clan heads' letter, if any, was not about the corruption of minds by 'outsiders' or about the caste being spoilt but the distance girls and boys had to travel to school and perhaps live away from home in harsh climatic conditions.

As far as this work is concerned, English suggests modernities, practices that communities negotiate, practices that are seen as liberating, more humane, more equal that drastically changed heretofore fixed structures—all of which to a considerable extent made possible by English and English education. The tensions between these existing and newer practices are much studied as conflicts between tradition and modernity. The resolution of tension between tradition and modernity, between the public and the private, between the material and spiritual, between the exterior and the interior and domestic, now known to us as colonial modernity, is fraught with gendered and casteist notions of the binaries involved. For most people outside the privileged realm, the dividing line between what was public and the private, what was exterior and interior was very thin if non-existent. Dilip Menon (2006, 134–135), has discussed how tradition that was considered spiritual and hence superior to the material world of the West was not accessible to the backward and lowered castes. Although Dilip Menon's argument is agreeable to an extent, 'accessibility' of tradition of the upper castes leaves no tradition of their own for the lower castes. It suggests there was one tradition which some could access who barred others from accessing it. For many communities, again, like Pandian drawing from Gowthaman (2002) points out in the conclusion to his article, tradition revolved around small-scale agriculture, hunting and gathering, sharing, collective living with little or no hierarchy, labouring for others, and cultural forms emerging from these materialistic and imaginations of creativity—that most of us need to be proud of.

> Gowthaman, one of the leading Tamil intellectuals and a Dalit literary critique, rejects the civilisational claims and the teleology of modernity, and instead recuperates the past of lowly hill cultivators, hunters, fisherpeople, pastoralists, and the like as the high point of human achievement. He characterises their social life as communal, with people pooling together and sharing food with a sense of equality, without much internal differentiation. (Pandian 2002, 1739)

This is true for most backward and lowered castes for whom labouring either for themselves or for the upper castes blurred and erased the binaries of outside and the inside. What one may construe as tradition was built around the practicalities of life that could maximize productivity in some form or other. Lives that were in no way certain led to fluid notions which were open to newness, minimizing conflict with outsiders, and welcoming changes that were seen as productive like the introduction of English.

Drawing from Menon, the community here is looked into in terms of resistance and negotiations with the existing unequal social order. This would enable a critique of nationalism's notion of a wider community of Hindus devoid of differentiating differences within and outside its fold. And following Aijaz Ahmad (1992) about how the discourse of nationalism has determined discussions on identity and cultural forms in the context of colonial and postcolonial India, I would argue that we need to look at these formations beyond the discourse of nationalism and anti-colonialism. For, as Sharmila Rege points out, drawing from Sumit Sarkar:

> the gains of the women's rights movements and the anticaste movements which had appropriated aspects of the colonial administration as resources would be completely lost in the binaries of the western and the indigenous. (Rege 2002, 1039)

From all these rendering the apparently simplistic argument that English ushered in simple necessities of life, and becomes a very powerful signifier. as Osella and Osella evocatively argue, towards 'progress' and in complicated ways, English worked and continues to work towards 'desired (happy) story-endings (40) and as Pandey writes:

> The matter of dreaming in English, which one might also describe as the dream of modernity and justice, requires greater historicisation and reflexivity, and fuller appreciation of the fact that the project of human freedom is premised on constant struggle, negotiation, creativity, rethinking and recreation. (59)

If this is a modernity that can be understood not necessarily as anticolonial, not framed by nationalist debates of the time, but as mobility involving no separation of material and the spiritual, it is also a progress that rides on ambiguities and tensions as mapped by Alok Mukherjee and Rita Kothari. If the gift of English worked to consolidate caste hegemonies, it also worked in countering this hegemony, a space of contest which Sanskrit or any other dominant language failed to provide, especially for people lowered in the caste order.[13] It countered the dominant modes of knowledge, of day-to-day practices, and also a sense of dignity in relation to people assumed to be higher up in the order.

## English Today and Our Tongues

My argument here is not whether Dalit–Bahujans all over the country use English to assert themselves. Writing about this in 1999, Anand points to how Dalits are writing in various tongues they are comfortable in.

> But this again does not mean that a Dalit from Andhra Pradesh is comfortable articulating his problems in 'standardised' Telugu—a Sanskritic Telugu that is prescribed by textbooks. Kancha Ilaiah, a Dalit-bahujan thinker from Andhra Pradesh, theorises, in English of the purposelessness of Dalit children being forced to acquire a culture that is alien to them through a language which is far removed from their social world—brahmanical bookish Telugu having nothing to do with the production-based materiality of the Dalits' Telugu. (Anand 1999, 2054–2056)

Sharan Kumar Limbale and Neerav Patel writing in Marathi and Gujarathi respectively, emphasize a similar point. This giving up of the standard language, touted as mother tongue is a step that needs a leap from the 'mother tongue' to the foster tongue, English as Kothari argues (61). Limbale elaborates:

> For their writing, Dalit writers have used the language of the quarters rather than the standard language. Standard language has a class. Dalit writers have rejected the class of this standard language. Cultured people in society consider standard language to be the proper language for writing. Dalit writers have rejected this validation of standard

---

[13] Note that there were contesting traditions/philosophies within Sanskrit but almost all who were involved were Brahmin men. English made this contesting ground much fairer and wider, way beyond a structure could withhold.

language by the cultured classes, because it is arrogant. To Dalit writers, the language of the basti [that is, settlement] seems more familiar than standard language. In fact, standard language does not include all the words of Dalit dialects. Besides, the ability to voice one's experience in one's mother tongue gives greater sharpness to the expression. (2004, 33–34)

I am indebted to Asha Singh who points to indigenous communities of the Northeast of India and people like Kodavas who have taken to English more than the 'regional/state/official language' are the communities that have skipped the casteist nature of standardized 'regional' languages thereby enabling a mobility for themselves that for most Dalit-Bahujans thus far has been difficult, steeped in dominant notions of language, culture, region they are associated with.

As I finish writing this, Peggy Mohan's wonderful book *Wanderers, Kings, Merchants* arrived. I do a quick read. Tracing languages from the Caribbean, Ireland, and India, Mohan, albeit arguing for a solid bilingual education, locates English in the context of elites and argues against it. The question of English for her rests in protecting the elite.

More important than any 'language problem' is the need to protect the elite and keep it separate and more entitled than everyone else. English is the perfect tool for apartheid. It sums up your family background in one go. (2021, 256)

This is of course true so far and also in line with what much of postcolonial scholarship has said about English. What this does not explain is the aspiration for English and neither does it explain a whole lot of ambivalences. As the preface to Saxena's new book tells us, 'the use of English by Modi and Rohith[14] conjures a vernacular English that is belied and buried under the rather flat narrative of global narrative' (2022, xvii). Hany Babu's attempt at understanding the ambivalence of English, which does not have a defined status in our official parlance (Associate

[14] Narendra Modi, India's current prime minister and Rohith Vemula, the research scholar from the University of Hyderabad whose death led to widespread anti-caste student movement in India.

Official Language that *was* to be dismantled in fifteen years from 1963) is illustrative.

> On the one hand, English is the invisible language to the framers of the Constitution except the allowance that it can continue to be used for all the purposes that it was used prior to the transfer of power (apart from the express provision to use it in the superior courts). On the other, it is not spelt out what the policy towards it should be in terms of promoting or not promoting it in education. While officially, English is treated as an invisible or untouchable language, it continues to dominate the public sphere and having no access to good English is often the determinants of social mobility, wherefore the underprivileged find it impossible to catch up as the state has no obligation to provide education in English for them. (2017, 117)

But precisely because English is an 'untouchable' language and a language without a caste memory unlike Sanskrit, and despite its elite nature connected to colonialism, English being outside the caste system that has influenced the official categorization of languages in India (in which the status of English is ambivalent), English stands outside this hierarchized structure of caste language nexus thereby offering a huge emancipatory potential for all.

To this potential of English, I would also add the potential of translation. Translation and translation into English has the potential not just to make texts and lives visible, of those that were thus far invisibilized. More importantly, 'trans', as in change, is a process heralded by English in very many ways, where people were translated by others and also self-translated into something else. Works from Dalits translated into English that carries forth the struggles, but also the ideals of equality, justice, freedom, and love as Sharan Kumar Limbale puts it in his *Towards an Aesthetic of Dalit Literature* is a solidarity that is transformative that is pan-Indian, universal.

> [H]undreds of thousands of people appear to be passionate about freedom, love, justice and equality. They have sacrificed themselves for these ideals. [ ... ] Equality, freedom, justice and love are the basic sentiments of people and society. [ ... ] There has never been a revolution

in the world for the sake of pleasure and beauty. Many governments have been overturned for equality, freedom and justice. This is history. The literature that glorifies pleasure gives central place to the pleasure-seeking aesthete. The literature that promotes equality, freedom and justice is revolutionary, and it emphasizes the centrality of the human being and society. If pleasure-giving literature arouses joy and sympathy in people, revolutionary literature awakens consciousness of self-respect. (2004, 119)

That this revolution is possible only via English translation, that connects, organizes at a much larger level, beginning from the times of Ambedkar, alongside other languages that organize at the immediate level. This is what Probal Dasgupta calls a *Transnation*. Drawing the idea both from a gender paradigm of transgender and translation, it defines transnation as a 'republic based explicitly on a recognition of ethnic multiplicity and on the constitutive use of translation within the republic (Dasgupta 2008, 1–2). Because these multiplicities are translated at every level and are also translated into English language and the ideals of liberation that the marginalized locate in English, tweaking Shankar's idea of translation-in-solidarity while questioning the translation-in-domination (2012: 156–157) seems to be transgressing boundaries that were for millenia formidable.

# References

Ahmad, Aijaz. 1992. *In Theory: Classes, Nations, Literature*. New Delhi: Oxford University Press.

Ambedkar. B. R. 1936. 'Annihilation of Caste'. https://ccnmtl.columbia.edu/projects/mmt/ambedkar/web/readings/aoc_print_2004.pdf

Ambedkar, B. R. 2002. 'Who were the Shudras?'. In *The Essential Writings of B. R. Ambedkar*, ed. Valerian Rodrigues, pp. 385–395. New Delhi: Oxford University Press.

Anand, S. 1999. 'Sanskrit, English and Dalits'. *Economic and Political Weekly* 34 (30): 2053–2056.

Babu, Hany. 2017. 'Breaking the Chaturvarna System of Languages The Need to Overhaul the Language Policy'. *Economic and Political Weekly* 52 (23): 112–119.

Chatterjee, Bankim Chandra. 2005 (1882). *Anandamath or The Sacred Brotherhood*, trans. Julius Lipner. New Delhi: Oxford University Press.

Chinnappa, Nadikerianda. 1924. *Pattole Palame*. Bengaluru: Kannada Pustaka Pradhikara.

Dasgupta, Probal. 2008. 'The Temper of my Familiarization: The Transnation and Its Counterpoints'. In *Narrating the Transnation: the Dialectics of Culture and Identity*, eds Krishna Sen and Sudeshna Chakravarti, pp. 25–37. Kolkata: Das Gupta and Amp. Co.

Ilaiah, Kancha. 2015. 'Dalits and English'. https://www.anveshi.org.in/Dalits-and-english/ Accessed 1 August 2021.

Joshi, Svati (ed.). 1991. *Rethinking English: Essays in Literature, Language, History*. New Delhi: Trianka.

Kothari, Rita. 2013. 'Cast(e) in a Caste-less language: English as a Language of "Dalit" Expression'. *Economic and Political Weekly* 48 (39): 60–68.

Limbale, Sharankumar. 2004. *Towards An Aesthetic of Dalit Literature: History, Controversies and Considerations*, trans. Alok Mukherjee. Hyderabad: Orient Longman.

Lindsay, A. W. C. 1871. *Report on the Coorg General Census of 1871*. Bangalore: Mysore Government Press.

Lipner, Julius. 2005 (1882). 'Introduction'. In Bankim Chatterjee, *Anandamath or The Sacred Brotherhood*, trans. Julius Lipner, p. 124. New Delhi: Oxford University Press.

Menon, Dilip. 2006. *The Blindness of Insight: Essays on Caste in Modern India*. Pondicherry: Navayana.

Mohan, Peggy. 2021. *Wanderers, Kings, Merchants. The Story of India Through its Languages*. Gurugram: Penguin Viking.

Mukherjee, Alok. 2009. *This Gift of English: English Education and the Formation of Alternative Hegemonies in India*. Hyderabad: Orient Blackswan.

Narzary, Raju. 2021. *The Bodos: A Revolutionary Journey*. Kokrajhar: Kokrajhar Literary Festival Reception Committee.

Niranjana, Tejaswini. 1990. 'Translation, Colonialism and Rise of English'. *Economic and Political Weekly* 25 (15): 773–779.

Osella, Caroline and Filippo Osella. 2004. 'Once a Upon a Time in the West: Narrating Modernity in Kerala, South India'. In *Culture and Modernity: Historical Explorations*, ed. K. N. Ganesh, pp. 39–73. Calicut: Calicut University Press.

Pandey, Gyanendra. 2016. 'Dreaming in English: Challenges of Nationhood and Democracy'. *Economic and Political Weekly* 51 (16): 56–62.

Pandian, M. S. S. 2002. 'One Step outside Modernity: Caste, Identity Politics and Public Sphere'. *Economic and Political Weekly* 37 (18): 1735–1741.

Pandian, M. S. S. 2008. 'Writing Ordinary Lives'. *Economic and Political Weekly* 43 (38): 34–40.

Pani, Susmit Prasad and Samar Kumar Pattnaik. 2006. *Vivekananda, Aurobindo and Gandhi on Education*. New Delhi: Amol Publications.

Phule, Savitribai. 1850. https://drambedkarbooks.com/2015/01/03/few-poems-by-savitribai-phule/ Accessed 13 November 2021.

Poonacha, Veena. 2002. *From the Land of a Thousand Hills: Portraits of Three Kodagu Women*. Mumbai: Sparrow.

Ramanujan, A. K. 1989. 'Is There an Indian Way of Thinking? An Informal Essay'. *Contributions to Indian Sociology* 23 (1): 41–58.

Rani, Suneetha K. 2017. *Influence of English on Indian Women Writers: Voices from Regional Languages*. New Delhi: Sage-Stree.

Rani, Suneetha K., Alladi Uma, and D. Murali Manohar. 2014. 'Introduction'. In *English in the Dalit Context*, eds. Alladi Uma, K. Suneetha Rani, and D. Murali Manohar, pp. 1–9. Hyderabad: Orient Blackswan.

Rege, Sharmila. 2002. 'Conceptualising Popular Culture "Lavani" and "Powada" in Maharashtra. *Economic and Political Weekly* 37 (11): 1038–1047.

Rice, Lewis. 1882. *Report on Education in Coorg: 1834–1882*. Calcutta: Indian Education Commission. Government of India.

Saxena, Akshya. 2022. *Vernacular English: Reading the Anglophone in Postcolonial India*. Princeton, NJ: Princeton University Press.

Scott, James. 2009. *The Art of Not Being Governed: An Anarchist History of Upland Southeast Asia*. Hyderabad: Orient Blackswan.

Shankar, S. 2012. *Flesh and Fish Blood: Postcolonialism, Translation and the Vernacular*. Berkeley and Los Angeles, CA: California University Press.

Sunder Rajan, Rajeshwari (ed.). 1992. *The Lie of the Land: English Literary Studies in India*. Delhi: Oxford University Press.

Tagore, Rabindranath. 2011 (1917). 'Nationalism in India'. In *Indian Philosophy in English: From Renaissance to Independence*, eds Nalini Bhushan and Jay L. Garfield, pp. 21–36. Delhi: Oxford University Press.

Tharakeshwar, V. B. 2014. 'Caste and Language: The Debate on English in India'. In *English in the Dalit Context*, eds Alladi Uma, K. Suneetha Rani, and D. Murali Manohar, pp. 169–180. Hyderabad: Orient Blackswan.

Tharu, Susie (ed.) 1998. *Subject to Change: Teaching Literature in the Nineties*. Hyderabad: Orient Longman.

Thirumal, P. 2021. 'Regurgitative Violence: The Sacred and the Profane in Higher Education Institutions in India'. *Economic and Political Weekly* 56 (23): 15–18.

Vishwanathan, Gauri. 1989. *Masks of Conquest: Literary Study and British Rule in India*. New York: Columbia University Press.

# Conclusion

## Mother Tongues

In late 2014, the then Ministry of Human Resources, now renamed the Ministry of Education, decided to stop teaching German, replacing it with Sanskrit in the Central Government-run Kendriya Vidyalaya schools. The following are parts of an open letter I had written to Ms Smriti Irani, minister of Human Resources, under whom this decision was taken. In 2014, my son went to a Kendriya Vidyalaya school in Hyderabad, the capital of the newly formed Telangana, where Telugu is spoken by the majority. The current focus on mother tongues by the New Education Policy 2020 of India makes this current discussion quite relevant.

I was indeed puzzled to know that the Kendriya Vidyalaya offered Hindi, Sanskrit, and German but no Telugu or any other living Indian tongue. Some time ago, I went to the school authorities and asked them about the absence of Telugu, especially since the three-language formula that they cite does mandate that all schools need to teach the 'local', 'regional' language/mother tongue. The answer was even more puzzling. If students or parents want Telugu to be taught, there needs to be a request from at least ten parents. What I did not understand is this—if teaching a 'local' language has to be requested, how come the teaching of Hindi and Sanskrit does not follow the same logic? But I have a more complicated question—what indeed is 'local'? Or what is one's 'mother tongue'? In Hyderabad, given its social geography, Urdu is equally local as is Telugu. Urdu was the medium of instruction for decades until the 1956 linguistic reorganization of states. Urdu implied culture and sophistication, had a 'proper' history and culture, and unlike Sanskrit was and is accessible to all. Urdu not only has a cultural history but also has a popular one so evident in cinema from Mumbai: it is Urdu cinema we consume not Hindi as has been pointed out so very often. So then, why not Urdu? What does

*Languages of Minority.* Sowmya Dechamma CC, Oxford University Press. © Oxford University Press 2024.
DOI: 10.1093/oso/9780198908456.003.0005

Sanskrit suggest that Urdu doesn't? Let's forget Urdu for the moment and ask what about other local languages that are not considered worthy enough to be included in the eighth schedule of the Indian Constitution[1] and modern enough to be called modern Indian languages? Telangana, where I now live, has many such languages pretty much like elsewhere in India. Banjara, Gondi, Konda, Kuvi, Chencu, and Koya, just to name a few. So, if the dominant local languages in Hyderabad is Urdu and Telugu, the local language in Adilabad should be Gondi among others. If children learn best in their mother tongue, why not in their own tongue? I mention these languages because my children do not have a single tongue: one is Kodava, a language of Kodagu from Karnataka; Telugu from their father; and English from everywhere. Kodava like the above languages mentioned does not become part of the list of languages desired in modern nation states. Historically, the idea of a mother tongue is a recent invention. Sumathy Ramaswamy, Shamsur Faruqi, and Lisa Mitchell have beautifully shown how mother tongues in the cases of Tamil, Urdu and Hindi, and Telugu respectively, have been built over a period of time, how the construction of a mother tongue is largely an intellectual and state enterprise, and how the idea of mother tongue is based on certain exclusionary strategies. In addition, G. N. Devy points out how dominant Indian languages like Hindi are constructed by census and the in national popular imagination as a mother tongue that subsumes a whole gamut of languages including Bhojpuri, Pahadi, Kumaoni, Awadhi, Bundeli, Maithili, and such.[2] More importantly, I mention these 'small' languages because I think there is a need to recover differences, a need to distinguish between lives practised and imagined histories that have supposedly bound us together. The People's Linguistic Survey of India[3] mentions that there are over 780 languages in India. Of these 780, around 210 languages belong to Northeast India. How many of us can even name two among these 210 rich, diverse, Northeastern languages? Why should one bother? It is 'they' who should know what is 'ours', not the other way round. Never in human history has

[1] The Eight Schedule of the Indian Constitution recognizes certain languages of India as Scheduled languages. Currently, of the hundreds of languages used in India, only 22 figure in the list.

[2] G. N. Devy. https://www.thehindu.com/opinion/lead/getting-the-language-count-right/article62111326.ece. Accessed 13 May 2021.

[3] http://www.peopleslinguisticsurvey.org/ Accessed 19 June 2021.

'who has to know what' been naïve and bereft of power. In such a scenario when it would be immensely worthwhile to explore ways to study these languages, why Sanskrit? Unlike German, Urdu, Hindi, Telugu, and indeed English, these languages do not have the factor of "usability" or a writable history. If German is foreign, so is English. What do we do with it now? Stretching a little further, Sanskrit is foreign to most Indians as well. But then, languages grow, die, borrow, give, evolve, get killed, and are erased constantly. A language like English which is not ours, can become ours either by direct or indirect forces of power. Aren't we proud of Tamil being one of the official languages of Singapore? Do we not gloat that Hindi, Bangla, Tamil, Sanskrit, and so on, are taught in America, Canada, Europe, and other places? That cinemas from India have an industry and market of their own in many parts of the world is of huge consequence for us not only in terms of profit but also in matters of cultural pride.

It is no wonder that a language like Sanskrit and the knowledge it carried that was so well guarded within the still unbreakable walls of caste practices died a natural death. Given the contemporary situation where it is mostly children of backward and lowered castes who attend government schools, whose histories have no memory of Sanskrit, isn't it ironic that what was once denied to them is now made mandatory, even when they do not want it? The upper classes and castes to whom Sanskrit can be said to have belonged now choose between French or German or Spanish in their private schools. Maybe we need to think a why the recovery of difference from very 'local' spaces becomes essential. Because it gives each one of us a space to claim as our own, because only then is there resistance to the merging of histories and spiritual symbols, because only then the indifference to histories of 'small' people with small languages can teach us many a thing—in schools or elsewhere.

The above is not just the case with Sanskrit. This linguistic nationalism, this chauvinism is very much part of almost all dominant languages of India, be it Tamil, Hindi, Kannada, Malayalam, Bangla, or even Assamese. Take, for example, the case from Assam:

> Tribes have often highlighted that the 'Assamese nationalism' discourse was narrow and rarely included other communities. However, Tribes such as the Misings, Deoris, Rabhas, etc. have still consistently supported the Assamese movement against the imposition of Bengali

language or Hindi in Assam. But in turn they now find themselves consistently marginalised, with their linguistic and cultural heritage derecognised by the State and the hegemonic forces. [ … ] the Home Ministry of Assam states that the government is also mulling over a separate legislation which will make only those who learned Assamese till their matriculation suitable for government jobs in Assam. These moves are clear indications of a non-inclusive homogenised Assamese nationalism taking precedence over the inclusion of minority linguistic and cultural aspirations. Such a move alienates various linguistic identities such as those of Tribes such as the Misings, Deoris and Rabhas, etc. and limits the definition of 'Axomiya' to just the speakers of the language.[4]

Connected to this is the issue of how many exams for central government jobs are conducted in Hindi apart from English, depriving learners and speakers of other languages employment. It is here that languages do not just imply a denial of cultural space, a cultural pride but implies a livelihood denied. This non-recognition of mother tongues, or in fact, the very limited understanding of what a mother tongue is has been an issue that has rarely been addressed in all its complexities either by academics or by policymakers. In effect, this idea of linguistic nationalism associated with cultural sophistication and material benefit is a template that is often used to retain the status quo of the dominant.

## Mother Tongue: Contentions

Perhaps it is apt to begin this discussion with what the Supreme Court of India has to say about mother tongue. Drawing from Article 350A, the answer by a panel of Constitution bench to the question 'what does mother tongue mean?' was the following:

> Mother tongue in the context of the Constitution would, therefore, mean the language of the linguistic minority in a State and it is the parent or the guardian of the child who will decide what the mother

---

[4] Manoranjan Pegu. 2020. https://www.thehindu.com/opinion/lead/striking-a-blow-against-assams-inclusive-ethos/article31965577.ece. Accessed 6 August 2021.

tongue of child is. The Constitution nowhere provides that mother tongue is the language which the child is comfortable with, and while this meaning of 'mother tongue' may be a possible meaning of the 'expression', this is not the meaning of mother tongue in Article 350A of the Constitution or in any other provision of the Constitution and hence we cannot either expand the power of the State or restrict a fundamental right by saying that mother tongue is the language which the child is comfortable with.[5]

Like the observations of the Supreme Court, debates around mother tongue have always been heated and forever contested. Even in the Court's observation and in popular perception, mother tongue has been largely an idea operating in the emotional realm without considerations of the livelihoods and practices associated and dissociated with and from languages. What exactly is mother tongue is a question that is highly charged and always debatable. Le Page argues that mother tongue is one of the strongest stereotypes, 'a cultural stereotype with many strong ideological implications varying from culture to culture (2020, 411) in the contemporary world and one that is invoked frequently by propagandists for vernacular education' (2020, 460), holds true for all contexts and regions across the world. This goes alongside the debates around what 'regional' and 'local' languages are. Is mother tongue a language spoken at home? What if there are many tongues spoken at home, which is the case in most of the border areas lying between many states that were linguistically organized only in the 1950s? What if parents and grandparents belong to different linguistic communities, caste communities, from different regions? What about children belonging to the many Adivasi communities numbering less than 10,000 and not counted in the official census? What about languages of the many Adivasi/Tribal communities that are subsumed under the 'regional' mother tongue category? Why is the 'regional' often associated with the mother tongue, even if it is not a child's spoken tongue at home? Once we posit Kannada (for example) as a regional language, does it imply that there are languages like Hindi (rarely English) that can take the position of the national language, albeit there being no

---

[5] https://indiankanoon.org/docfragment/139768401/?big=3&formInput=article%20350A. Accessed 19 June 2020.

constitutional category in India called the national language and indeed regional language? Every language is a regional language spoken in specific regions of the world at times that cuts across recently made linguistic boundaries. In this understanding, every language is also local. English and before that Latin and Sanskrit were languages of empires and religious establishments that travelled with the empire, with religion (and arts associated with them), and then capitalism and colonialism, each having many histories that need to be charted. English is indeed a mother tongue and also a local/native language for many, unlike Latin and Sanskrit which in recent histories are not anyone's mother tongue. When it comes to the present language scenario, even the census documents point to how one should not make connections between mother tongues (languages spoken at home) with categories of religion, language, and dialect.[6] Regional language is more often than not the dominant language of the state, a language which is included in the scheduled language list of India. In this unwritten hierarchy, Hindi stands as the unofficial national language, English as the untouchable associated official language (Hany Babu), the languages of the state as regional and scheduled, and all other languages that are not regional, not scheduled as 'local' or as dialects.

It is also observed that most speakers of these hundreds of languages often return the dominant language of the region as their mother tongue during language census—the main reason being that no value is attached to their own tongue and also because of the categorization of languages by governmental institutions and practices like that of education and census. Hany Babu, quoting Anvita Abbi, points to this non-recognition of mother tongues:

[S]peakers of a language in the absence of their language being recognised for education purposes, try to identify themselves with the dominant regional language speakers and at best retain their respective tongues only in the home domain. What is more alarming is that in many instances children are discouraged and at times punished for using their mother tongues even at home. According to Abbi, '[t]he sense of pride in associating with the dominant regional language is

considered as a step towards merging with the mainstream'. (quoted in
Babu 2017, 117)

This imagined sense of pride in identifying with the dominant regional is
what Asha Singh refers to as hindering the marginalizing from aspiring
and moving towards a social equal beyond the gender–caste–language
nexus that binds the regional.[7] Despite the last language census of India
carried out in 2011 having observations and instructions regarding what
can be considered mother tongue, the above practice is prevalent across
the country.

> Mother tongue is the language spoken in childhood by the person's
> mother to the person. If the mother died in infancy, the language mainly
> spoken in the person's home in childhood will be the mother tongue.
> In the case of infants and deaf mutes, the language usually spoken by
> the mother should be recorded. In case of doubt, the language mainly
> spoken in the household may be recorded. (4–5)[8]

But then, there are variations of course. In 1961, the language census
was for the first time enumerated in full and it returned 1,652 mother
tongues. G. N. Devy points to how in 1971, there was a change in logic
and this figure turned to 109 mother tongues. In 2011, the figures for
mother tongues from the language census is 19,569. In addition, the
census places some fifty-six languages as 'mothertongues' (Awadhi,
Bajjika, Bundeli, also 'others', etc.,) under the language 'Hindi'. These fifty
six 'mother tongues' are not eligible to the status of a language but are
subsumed under Hindi in the census.

Based on previous linguistic and sociological information, the authorities decided that of these, 18,200 did not match 'logically' with known
information. A total of 1,369 names—technically called 'labels'—were
picked as 'being names of languages'. In addition to the 1,369 'mother
tongue' names shortlisted, there were 1,474 other mother tongue names.
These were placed under the generic label 'Others'. As far as the census

---

[7] Like in the previous chapter, conversations with Asha Singh have contributed to this idea
greatly.
[8] https://censusindia.gov.in/2011Census/Language-2011/General%20Note.pdf. Accessed 22
January 2021.

is concerned, these linguistic 'Others' are not seen to be of any concern. The classification system has not been able to identify what or which languages these are and have been silenced by an innocuous label slapped on them.[9]

My intention is not to arrive at an understanding of mother tongue that is acceptable to all, but only to say how classifications of languages have always been burdened with notions associated with power, official or otherwise. The official categories of scheduled and non-scheduled languages, classical languages, have more to do with expansion of the idea of a nation than in empowering people and their livelihoods. In effect, these notions are carried forward into the education system where children who study in the 'regional' language, the dominant language of the region to be more specific, are associated with cultural history and pride, with merit and of course employability—all of which are disassociated from the child's mother tongue if it is different from the dominant regional language.

However, it is not just these two scheduled languages that are privileged (Hindi and English). A privilege of a lesser sort is enjoyed even by the other scheduled languages as they can be 'alternative media for the All India and Higher Central Services Examinations' as per the Official Languages Act 15. It is the non-scheduled languages that have none of these privileges. Many of the minor languages belonging to the Austro–Asiatic and Tibeto–Burman families are out of this scenario due to the emphasis on the major languages like Hindi, English, and Sanskrit. According to Agnihotri (2015), millions of children who speak these languages such as Angami, Santhali, Ao, Saura, or Bodo are forced to study through languages that are completely unknown to them and when they cannot understand the content of science or social sciences because of linguistic difficulty, they are dubbed as dull and incompetent (116).

This argument, similar to what is quoted in the previous chapter from Ilaiah, aims at pointing out two things. Firstly, that education in the dominant language of the region is often standardized, and Sanskritized to such an extent that it alienates children who cannot associate with the textualized form of language even when it is technically the same

---

[9] https://www.thehindu.com/opinion/lead/getting-the-language-count-right/article24454570.ece. Accessed 17 April 2021.

language. Secondly, as pointed above, the language in the classroom is either English in private schools and the dominant official language of the states in state government-run schools. This dominant state language is frequently not the mother tongue or the tongue spoken at home. It is either a different language or a standardized dialect far removed from the language spoken at home. Like in the previous chapters, the argument here is not for an education system that is exclusively in the perceived mother tongue. Nowhere in India can we perhaps find a classroom where all students speak the same language. The argument here is for an education that is imparted in the medium of English with various languages of the region, big and small, made available to children from the moment they start school. These languages, taught at schools like Kancha Ilaiah mentions, need to bring in the sociocultural ambience of the home and of their surroundings in non-standardized forms, in ways so that children can connect and value what is theirs. Scholars like Madhava Prasad argue that the whole purpose of education is meaningless if the language of instruction is English, which is still accessible largely to the elite, and that is not the language of the political commons. But what then is the language of political commons if one cannot articulate politics in one's own tongue? A standardized 'local' language that is dominant and removed from the daily lives of people, like the example Prasad quotes from—the diglossic nature of Arabic that has separated people from the classical, official Arabic used for governance? Babu complicates this further.

> At the regional level, the asymmetry between the scheduled and non-scheduled languages is leading not only to loss of cultural diversity, but is also leading to the hegemony of the regional elite. If the attempt to create a linguistically homogeneous people has not succeeded at the macro level of the nation, it seems to have had considerable success at the micro level of the region thanks to the linguistic reorganisation of the states. (2017, 115)

## Lastly...

I live in Hyderabad and I am from Kodagu, Karnataka. One of the first questions many of my Kannada-speaking friends ask my children when they first meet them is—oh! you do not know Kannada? It hardly matters that the children know Kodava, Telugu, and English. The assumption here is that there is a larger mother tongue than the tongue that is spoken at home by the mother. Indeed, this is how the idea of mother tongue emerged, by connecting the spoken tongues to the larger idea of motherland, mother Mary, and mother tongue.

To me, Ivan Illich is very perceptive in his ideas of how capitalism and nation state in Europe invented a mother tongue for its subjects. In India, this is combined with caste community and colonialism. Teaching of the mother tongue is the first invented part of universal education. In one of the world's best contradictions, mother tongue, a tongue that one is supposed to imbibe from the environment one inhabits now becomes a 'subject' that requires learning outside that environment.[10] This in itself proves how the 'mother tongue' taught in the formal setting of schools or any other institution is perceived as different, perceived as cultured and civilized unlike the speech forms spoken at one's home, and therefore requires training.

Tracing the 'birth' of mother tongue in Europe, Illich elaborates on how from the time the term was first used, mother tongue never meant the vernacular, but was always its contrary. Mother tongue as a term was first used by Catholic monks around eleventh century in Gorz, now in France to:

> designate a particular language they used, instead of Latin, when speaking from the pulpit. No Indo-Germanic culture before had used the term. The word was introduced into Sanskrit in the 18th Century as a translation from English. The term has no roots in other major language families now spoken.[11]

Analysing the very interesting turn and connections of mother tongue to religious and nation state's history, Illich points out how this very mystical, invisible mother becomes essential for salvation. It is this tongue of the mother that arose as a territorial claim of the Abbey of Gorz in

---

[10] Ivan Illich. http://www.davidtinapple.com/illich/1980_vernacular_values.html. Accessed 12 September 2018.
[11] Illich, Ibid.

the eleventh century that becomes inseparable from the Mother Church and Mother Mary. The manner in which Mother Church paved the way to Motherland and thereby cementing Mother Tongue's connection to the mystic reality of Church–Land–Goddess–Tongue ironically controlled by males becomes the foundation of most nation states—is Illich's contribution to the history of mother tongue that has not really been recognized. Whether it is Latin or Sanskrit, that there can be no salvation without the services provided by the priest, who could only invoke these languages of God, who becomes the mother, is something to take note of. Also important to take note of is the huge difference: the manner in which the Church changed its languages to include 'mother tongues', after twelfth-century Gorz, with its later development associated with capitalist print industry, colonialism, and translation of Bible, thereby giving rise to the proliferation of written languages and simultaneously a reading public (through religion) that hitherto had little access to reading or writing. In the caste Hindu world, until the present, Sanskrit has retained the exclusive passage to God and mostly through the Brahmin men, with few exceptions in the last few decades. The difference lies in this: Sanskrit has retained its religious territory and also its privileged connection to the caste that held power over it. Although Sanskrit is mandatory (if otherwise it is Hindi, Sanskrit mother's legitimized daughter) and is imposed in central government schools, and contemporary cultural nationalism has maintained Sanskrit's glory popularized by European orientalists; that the literary and political territory it once held has undergone subversive changes and this ironically happens with the rise of vernaculars, is a crucial point to be noted following Sheldon Pollock.

In countries like India, which especially have built their nationalist ideology in apparent opposition to European cultural identities, the notion of mother tongue has become so sacrosanct that to say the idea was non-existent until translated from English in the eighteenth century seems blasphemous. For a considerable section of people in India who love to point all their ills to colonialism, it is strange that we need to subscribe to the very European notion—one country, one language, tracing the mother to one single language, Sanskrit—however factually flawed this notion is. The idea that a language represents a nation is one of colonialism's gifts to us. So is the idea of the nation state. The complex process of modern nation-building of colonial countries saw a need to be represented as one cultural entity. What best can a country claim as its continued history, continued culture other than its language, especially in its written form? It is this need for a cultural continuity that stood for a unique, great past, in which language and literature became necessary for almost all European nations and subsequently to nations they colonized. Despite the existence of many languages, many dialectal differences, and many contestations, European nations have, through a very elite and exclusionary process, adopted a national language which today is being contested from different corners including by immigrants from India. There are exceptions like Switzerland, Belgium, and recently Singapore which have far long been relatively stable countries without ever having a single national language. How ironic then that the Indian nationalists' animosity towards English makes us blind to the fact that it is English that gave us the idea of a singular nation: one nation, one language. Nowhere in the history of the subcontinent was there a need to showcase its unity through one language or one culture until after colonialism and this one language is touted as everybody's mother tongue is the mother of all ironies.

We need to operate and function and exert our agencies in a contextual manner, in a manner that makes most sense to our immediate environs.[12] Local is often the site where social hierarchies manifest the strongest. Not all binaries of language operate at once, at all sites. Like Hany Babu points out, the Indian Constitution and the main players in the official language debate in constituent assembly failed to envisage a multilingual situation for a nascent nation state (113). Of course, now, the parallel is between the linguistic hierarchy and the caste system—by positing Sanskrit as occupying a privileged position and English (which is a rank outsider in the constitutional scheme) as a language with emancipatory capacity due to its positioning outside the legitimized hierarchy (Babu 2017, 113) Speakers of 'Hindi' rarely learn any other language of India other than English, which is also limited when compared to speakers of other languages, in systems of skewed learning. Speakers of other scheduled languages need to learn English and/or Hindi. It is ironic that all speakers

---

[12] Akeel Bilgrami. https://www.thehindu.com/opinion/op-ed/september-11-a-brief-personal-reflection/article36421240.ece. Accessed 9 April 2021.

of non-scheduled languages would be doubly burdened, as apart from Hindi or English, they would also be forced to acquire proficiency in the dominant language/ regional language of the state (that is, in the states where Hindi is not the language of the state (Babu 2017, 115). This says a lot about the status, recognition and non-institutionalizing of the glorified mother tongue.

Following Bilgrami and Hany Babu, I argue that we need to see what works at the local, micro level and also how this can be connected to the various sociopolitical structures we are part of. We need a system wherein a child, an individual can grow uninhibited, valuing everything within and around while simultaneously paving the way for building connections with the larger world. Given all the contradictions, this can be done only when everyone's mother tongue becomes the medium through which they access the world in English.

I would like to end with a quote from Gyanendra Pandey's 'Dreaming in English' towards a politics that needs to recognize our local work with all tongues alongside English:

In the end, Mohandas Gandhi and Ta-Nehisi Coates may speak the same language as the theorist of the mestiza, even if their vocabulary is a little different: 'Soy un amasamiento, I am an act of kneading, of uniting and joining that not only has produced both a creature of darkness and a creature of light, but also a creature that questions the definitions of light and dark and gives them new meanings'. And, while ruling classes and their apologists will scarcely admit it, perhaps that is what the better part of dreaming in English—the dream of freedom and democracy in the twentieth and twenty-first centuries—has always been about. (Pandey 62)

# References

Babu, Hany. 2017. 'Breaking the Chaturvarna System of Languages. The Need to Overhaul the Language Policy'. *Economic and Political Weekly* 52 (23): 112–119.

Bilgrami, Akeel. 2021. 'A Brief Personal Reflection'. https://www.theHindu.com/opinion/op-ed/september-11-a-brief-personal-reflection/article36421240.ece. Accessed 2 May 2022.

Dechamma, Sowmya C. C. 2014. 'On Teaching Sanskrit and Mother Tongues'. *Economic and Political Weekly* 49 (47).

Devy, G. N. 2018. 'Getting the Language Count Right'. https://www.theHindu.com/opinion/lead/getting-the-language-count-right/article62111326.ece. Accessed 12 September 2021.

Faruqi, Shamsur Rahman. 2001. *Early Urdu Literary Culture*. New Delhi: Oxford University Press.

Ilaiah, Kancha. 2015. 'Dalits and English'. https://www.anveshi.org.in/Dalits-and-english/, pp. 9–10. Accessed 1 August 2021.

Illich, Ivan. 1980. 'Vernacular Values'. http://www.davidtinapple.com/illich/1980_vernacular_values.html, pp. 1–37.Accessed 12 September 2018.

Le Page, Robert B. 2020. *Language and Identity. Selected Papers of Robert B. Le Page*, eds Rama Kant Agnihotri, Mahendra Kishore Verma, and Vandana Puri. Hyderabad: Orient Blackswan.

Mitchell, Lisa. 2009. *Language, Emotion, and Politics in South India: The Making of a Mother Tongue*. Ranikhet: Permanent Black.

Pandey, Gyanendra. 2016. 'Dreaming in English: Challenges of Nationhood and Democracy'. *Economic and Political Weekly* 51 (16): 56–62.

Pegu, Manoranjan. 2020. 'Striking a Blow against Assam's Inclusive Ethos' https://www.theHindu.com/opinion/lead/striking-a-blow-against-assams-inclusive-ethos/article31965577.ece. Accessed 6 August 2021.

Pollock, Sheldon. 2006. *The Language of the Gods in the World of Men*. Delhi: Permanent Black.

Prasad, Madhava. 2014. 'The Political Commons: Language and the Nation State Form'. *Critical Quarterly* 56 (3): 92–105.

Ramaswamy, Sumathy. 1997. *Passions of the Tongue: Language Devotion in Tamil India, 1891–1970*. Berkeley, CA: University of California Press.

# Index